What *Investor's Business Daily* R
"Leaders & Success" Section

I am a mentor to a young boy, 13, who has no Dad. I have met with him weekly for three years. I use the "Leaders & Success" section to develop messages for him that he can apply to his benefit. That this is working is no surprise I am sure, for as we think so we are. But now that several of his friends have joined in these discussions it has been doubly gratifying.

— Michael Burton

"Leaders & Success" is an important part of my mornings. It is an inspirational tool that I utilize not only to assure that I begin my days on a positive note, but it gives me food for thought.

— Jim Elder

My daughter in the 5th grade reads a "Leaders & Success" bio from *Investor's Business Daily* every day as I drive her to school. What an education she is getting.

— Michael McLennan

"Leaders & Success" is read by my 15-year-old and his friends daily. Keep up the good work.

— Peter Siracusa

I love the "Leaders & Success" section as it gives inspiration to me to go ahead in my life and to think about life in a positive and successful way.

— Veera Reddy

Other McGraw-Hill Books by William J. O'Neil

The Successful Investor: What 80 Million People Need to Know to Invest Profitably and Avoid Big Losses

How to Make Money in Stocks: A Winning System in Good Times or Bad

24 Essential Lessons for Investment Success: Learn the Most Important Investment Techniques from the Founder of Investor's Business Daily

Business Leaders & Success

55 Top Business Leaders & How They Achieved Greatness

Introduction by William J. O'Neil

McGraw-Hill

New York   Chicago   San Francisco   Lisbon   London
Madrid   Mexico City   Milan   New Delhi   San Juan
Seoul   Singapore   Sydney   Toronto

Copyright © 2004 by William J. O'Neil. All rights reserved. Printed in the United States of America. Except as permitted under the United States Copyright Act of 1976, no part of this publication may be reproduced or distributed in any form or by any means, or stored in a database or retrieval system, without the prior written permission of the publisher.

12 13 14 15 16 DOC/DOC 0 9 8 7 6 5 4 3 2

ISBN: 0-07-142680-9

McGraw-Hill books are available at special quantity discounts to use as premiums and sales promotions, or for use in corporate training programs. For more information, please write to the Director of Special Sales, Professional Publishing, McGraw-Hill, Two Penn Plaza, New York, NY 10121-2298. Or contact your local bookstore.

Library of Congress Cataloging-in-Publication Data

Business leaders & success : 55 top business leaders & how they achieved greatness / with an introduction from William J. O'Neil.—1st ed.
    p.   cm.
Includes index.
  ISBN 0-07-142680-9 (acid free)
  1. Success in business. 2. Businessmen. 3. Executives.
I. Title: Profiles in business success. II. O'Neil, William J.
III. Investor's business daily.
  HF5386.I55 2003
  658.4'09—dc21

2003013889

Contents

Credits

"Nike Co-founder Bill Bowerman: His Innovations For Runners Helped Build An Empire," by Marilyn Much, was originally published in *Investor's Business Daily* on January 24, 2000.

"Animator Walt Disney: His Innovation And Persistence Gave Birth To Magic," by J. Barnes, was originally published in *Investor's Business Daily* on October 24, 2000.

"Media Innovator Oprah Winfrey: Staying Positive Helped Her Climb To The Top," by Curt Schleier, was originally published in *Investor's Business Daily* on September 1, 1999.

"Industrialist Andrew Carnegie: His Innovations Led The U.S. Into The Steel Age," by Curt Schleier, was originally published in *Investor's Business Daily* on December 8, 1999.

"Publisher Katharine Graham: She Built Her Career On Persistence And Integrity," by Christopher L. Tyner, was originally published in *Investor's Business Daily* on July 24, 2001.

"Applied Materials' James Morgan: Listening To Employees Kept His Company Growing," by Christopher L. Tyner, was originally published in *Investor's Business Daily* on June 27, 2000.

"Hewlett-Packard's Carly Fiorina: How A Philosophy Major Came To Drive Technology's Big Engines," by Sylvia Tiersten, was originally published in *Investor's Business Daily* on March 4, 1999.

"Cosmetics Queen Mary Kay Ash: She Made Beauty A Big Seller," by Curt Schleier, was originally published in *Investor's Business Daily* on July 29, 2002.

"Self-Help Pioneer Dale Carnegie: He Won Friends And Influenced Many People," by Sean Higgins, was originally published in *Investor's Business Daily* on October 24, 2001.

"NBA Commissioner David Stern: He Pumped Up League Into An Entertainment Powerhouse," by Curt Schleier, was originally published in *Investor's Business Daily* on March 11, 1999.

"Wal-Mart Founder Sam Walton: He Learned From Competitors And Then Went His Own Way," by Katie Sweeney, was originally published in *Investor's Business Daily* on June 30, 1999.

"Paychex's Thomas Golisano Built Business By Hiring For Guts Instead Of Know-How," by David Price, was originally published in *Investor's Business Daily* on July 28, 1997.

"McDonald's Ray Kroc: He Cooked Up A Winner," by Curt Schleier, was originally published in *Investor's Business Daily* on October 25, 2001.

"Tupperware's Brownie Wise: Built and Prepped Her Army With Methodical Goal Setting," by Peter Krass, was originally published in *Investor's Business Daily* on August 28, 1998.

"Radio Shack's Charles Tandy: His Commonsense Approach Built An Electronics Giant," by Curt Schleier, was originally published in *Investor's Business Daily* on December 7, 2000.

"Retailer Charles R. Walgreen Sr.: His Innovations Helped Build Nation's Biggest Drugstore Chain," by David Saito-Chung, was originally published in *Investor's Business Daily* on July 21, 1999.

"Barney Creator Sheryl Leach: She Relied On Common Sense To Help Her Build A Purple Empire," by Donna Shew, was originally published in *Investor's Business Daily* on July 29, 1999.

"Bank Of America's A. P. Giannini: His Focus On Ordinary People Helped Build A Financial Goliath," by Curt Schleier, was originally published in *Investor's Business Daily* on December 16, 1999.

"Chewing Gum Mogul William Wrigley Jr.: He Stuck To His Vision," by Steve Watkins, was originally published in *Investor's Business Daily* on December 5, 2001.

"Organizer Nancy Brinker: Her Determination Helped Foundation Spread The Word," by Amy Reynolds, was originally published in *Investor's Business Daily* on June 1, 1999.

"Aviation Pioneer William Boeing: In Building His Empire, He Bowed To Just One Authority," by Anna Bray Duff, was originally published in *Investor's Business Daily* on January 28, 1998.

"AmeriCredit's Michael Barrington: Attitude Put Him In Driver's Seat Of Auto Loan Titan," by Christopher L. Tyner, was originally published in *Investor's Business Daily* on February 26, 2001.

"Nvidia's Jen-Hsun Huang: His Laserlike Focus Helps Keep His Company On Top," by James DeTar, was originally published in *Investor's Business Daily* on June 12, 2001.

"Entrepreneur Daisy Braxton: How She Used Her Fall Into Welfare To Reach Higher Than She Ever Had," by James V. O'Connor, was originally published in *Investor's Business Daily* on February 24, 1999.

"IGT's Charles Mathewson: Relationship-Building Helped Him Win Big," by Murray Coleman, was originally published in *Investor's Business Daily* on July 26, 2001.

"Tellabs' Michael Birck: Brashness Got Him Started, Tempering It Moved Him Up," by Adrienne Fox, was originally published in *Investor's Business Daily* on August 14, 1997.

"Electronics Maker Konosuke Matsushita: His Focus On Vision Boosted Him To The Top," by Michael Lyster, was originally published in *Investor's Business Daily* on August 17, 1999.

"*Ebony*'s John H. Johnson: How He Went From A Tin-Roof Shack To The Forbes 400," by John Berlau, was originally published in *Investor's Business Daily* on March 26, 1998.

"Home Depot's Arthur Blank And Bernie Marcus: They Rose To The Top By Putting Customers First," by Curt Schleier, was originally published in *Investor's Business Daily* on July 8, 1999.

"Juniper's Scott Kriens: Willingness To Learn Helped Him Build A Top Networker," by Steve Watkins, was originally published in *Investor's Business Daily* on December 11, 2000.

"Executive Ann Fudge: Relies On Lessons Of Youth To Keep Business Growing," by Curt Schleier, was originally published in *Investor's Business Daily* on June 7, 1999.

"Coca-Cola's Robert Woodruff: He Made The Real Thing," by David Saito-Chung, was originally published in *Investor's Business Daily* on November 12, 2001.

"Entrepreneur Michael Dell: How He Made His Firm The Fastest-Growing Computer Maker," by Nick Turner, was originally published in *Investor's Business Daily* on March 1, 1999.

"Nokia's Jorma Ollila: With Innovation And Insight, He Made His Company No. 1," by Christopher L. Tyner, was originally published in *Investor's Business Daily* on February 14, 2000.

"Harley-Davidson's Jeffrey Bleustein: Communication Focus Keeps His Company Roaring," by Marilyn Much, was originally published in *Investor's Business Daily* on February 28, 2001.

"*Sesame Street*'s Joan Ganz Cooney: The ABCs Of Creating A Classic," by Michael Mink, was originally published in *Investor's Business Daily* on February 7, 2003.

"SEI Investments' Alfred P. West Jr.: Amid Success, He Rededicated Company To Coping With Change," by Jed Graham, was originally published in *Investor's Business Daily* on October 5, 2000.

"eBay's Meg Whitman: Why This Dot-Com Keeps Growing," by Cord Cooper, was originally published in *Investor's Business Daily* on November 15, 2002.

"AOL's Steve Case: He Built An Online Empire By Keeping The Customer In Mind," by Pete Barlas, was originally published in *Investor's Business Daily* on February 10, 2000.

"Gap Inc. CEO Mickey Drexler: His Focus Made Customer Service More Than A Slogan," by Curt Schleier, was originally published in *Investor's Business Daily* on January 25, 2000.

"Starbucks' Howard Schultz: Keeping His Passion As Fresh As The Morning Coffee," by Matt Krantz, was originally published in *Investor's Business Daily* on February 2, 1999.

"IBM's Linda Sanford: Her Attention To Detail Put Her On The Fast Track," by Matt Krantz, was originally published in *Investor's Business Daily* on May 24, 1999.

"99 Cents Only Stores' David Gold: He Ignored Status Quo To Break New Retailing Ground," by David Saito-Chung, was originally published in *Investor's Business Daily* on June 19, 2000.

"Entrepreneur Madame C. J. Walker: She Used Marketing Savvy And Determination To Win Customers," by James V. O'Connor, was originally published in *Investor's Business Daily* on December 10, 1998.

"Master Of Advertising David Ogilvy: He Built On Quality," by Curt Schleier, was originally published in *Investor's Business Daily* on January 3, 2002.

"Cisco Systems' John Chambers: He Makes Sure The Customer Is Always First," by Michele Hostetler, was originally published in *Investor's Business Daily* on June 2, 1999.

"eBay Founder Pierre Omidyar: His Devotion To Community Created A Global Auction House," by Jennifer Lloyd, was originally published in *Investor's Business Daily* on August 20, 2001.

"Innovators Ole And Bess Evinrude: Their Resolve And Integrity Launched Millions Of Outboard Motors," by Sonja Carberry, was originally published in *Investor's Business Daily* on July 6, 1999.

"Statistician W. Edwards Deming: His Push For High Quality Changed The Corporate Approach," by Christopher L. Tyner, was originally published in *Investor's Business Daily* on November 20, 2000.

"Fashion Designer Coco Chanel: She Sewed Up Success," by Sarah Z. Sleeper, was originally published in *Investor's Business Daily* on October 26, 2001.

"Innovator Joseph C. Wilson: His Determination Built Xerox Into A Billion-Dollar Company," by Curt Schleier, was originally published in *Investor's Business Daily* on November 8, 2000.

"Inventor John Mauchly: His Determination Helped Launch The Computer Age," by Brian Deagon, was originally published in *Investor's Business Daily* on July 25, 2001.

"Inventor Howard Head: His Determination Revolutionized The Way We Ski And Play Tennis," by David Saito-Chung, was originally published in *Investor's Business Daily* on September 4, 2001.

"Intel Co-founder Robert Noyce: He Invented His Way To The Top," by Curt Schleier, was originally published in *Investor's Business Daily* on November 5, 2001.

"GE's Jack Welch: His Innovation Sealed The Company's Success," by Christopher L. Tyner, was originally published in *Investor's Business Daily* on October 31, 2000.

The majority of these articles have been updated for this collection.

Introduction

Successful people in all fields share similar qualities that move them to the top — desire, determination and drive, for instance. Yet they each have a different approach that gives them a unique edge.

Investor's Business Daily's "Leaders & Success" section tells you exactly how these people became successful, so you can apply their tips, traits and experiences to your life. Every one of these leaders has a story with lessons we can learn from.

In this collection of *Business Leaders & Success,* you'll learn why Sam Walton only opened Wal-Marts in small towns and avoided all big competitors, why he marked up his inventory less than his competitors and how he eventually outstripped those competitors to become the world's largest discount retailer. See how young Mary Kay Ash overcame the early hardship of having a sick father, and later a direct sales career hemmed in by a glass ceiling, only to go on and found her own highly successful cosmetics company. Discover how David Ogilvy began as a cook and then a pollster, and later developed his new ad agency into a giant organization. Find out what Joe Wilson did in the 1950s and 60s to make Xerox a top-performer when consultants and test markets found little interest in the new Xerox dry copier. And learn what Meg Whitman does today to keep eBay growing.

One characteristic you'll discover that all great leaders have in common is a positive attitude that gives them daily inspiration to meet challenges and overcome unforeseen obstacles. They don't get mired down in what went wrong. Great leaders choose to take the most positive approach to what many people would perceive as a huge problem; they fix it, work around it or figure out how to turn that "problem" into a solution.

When A. P. Giannini's bank burned down after the San Francisco earthquake and fire of 1906, he immediately set up a card table on the corner and loaned money — when no one else would — to merchants who all lost their businesses and had no collateral after the disaster. That's how Bank of America began.

And do you know who founded Home Depot? Two friends who'd just been fired from another hardware chain. They turned that negative experience into a positive one by putting their vision of an all-in-one giant hardware store into action.

Disneyland was also born out of a negative set of circumstances. Walt Disney's wife, brother and business partners all refused to invest any money in Walt's new idea to create a theme park dedicated to fun and happiness. Did he let all these naysayers hold him back? Of course, not! He founded a separate company to develop Disneyland and started a highly successful TV show, *The Wonderful World of Disney*, to help finance it.

These are just a few of the amazing facts you'll read about the business leaders in this collection. Avid readers *can* become leaders, and by studying how others have built successful careers, you, too, can get a giant head start on the path to leadership and success.

Everyone wants success at something, and the following 55 stories of unparalleled, entrepreneurial success offer ideas and guidelines that can help you make your desires and dreams a reality. We hope they inspire you the way they continue to inspire us.

Acknowledgments

No book finds its way into the hands of readers without the teamwork and dedication of many hardworking individuals. In particular, I am grateful to Deirdre Abbott, Sally Doyle, Sue Frazer, Cynthia Martin, Ken Shreve and Susan Warfel of *Investor's Business Daily*, and Donya Dickerson and Jane Palmieri of McGraw-Hill, for their excellent and thoughtful contributions to this highly inspirational book. And I especially wish to thank Shana Smith and Joannè von Alroth for their diligence, dedication and superb editorial guidance.

William J. O'Neil
Founder of *Investor's Business Daily*

PART I

Striving To Be The Best

1

Nike Co-founder
Bill Bowerman

His Innovations For Runners Helped
Build An Empire

Track coach Bill Bowerman was eating breakfast one morning in 1971 when his wife, Barbara, opened the waffle iron to pour another serving.

He constantly looked for ways to help his athletes improve. Then it hit him. If he mixed synthetic rubber, poured it into the back of the waffle iron and let it cool, he could make a better sole for a running shoe.

It took some grunting and wrenching with pliers to get the rubber off, wrote Bowerman, co-founder of Nike Inc., in *Guideposts* magazine in January 1988. But when he finally did, he'd come up with the first lightweight outsole, the Waffle sole, which revolutionized the running shoe. Today, every athletic shoemaker uses a waffle sole or some variation on everything from running to hiking shoes.

Bowerman (1911–99), the head track-and-field coach at the University of Oregon in Eugene from 1948 to 1972, was hugely competitive and at the same time fascinated with physiology. In studying the dynamics of running, he saw that the shoes runners used were cumbersome.

In the late 1950s, he devised a shoe with a heel wedge, better support and lighter sole. One problem: He couldn't find a company to make it. Though disappointed, Bowerman was inspired by a message he often used with his teams.

"Losing," he would say, "can be a real beginning."

He decided to make the shoes himself. Bowerman tested his designs on his team members, including Phil Knight, now Nike's chairman and chief executive. After that, Bowerman would sit in his garage and tinker with the shoe designs, which his team members gladly wore.

He figured others would be happy to have the shoes, too. In 1964, he and Knight teamed up to found Blue Ribbon Sports Inc. In 1972, the duo started the Nike brand for Bowerman's shoes. That year, four of the top seven finishers in the Olympic marathon wore Nikes.

The company name was changed to Nike Inc. in 1980, when it went public. It passed the billion-dollar revenue mark in 1986. Nike, based in Beaverton, Ore., markets its products in more than 100 countries and is the world's No. 1 sports and fitness company in market share and sales, about $9 billion in 2000. At that time, Nike accounted for more than 40% of all athletic-shoe sales in the United States.

Bowerman's inspiration and high standards had a lot to do with Nike's rise to stardom.

"Bowerman had a laser focus to solve a problem with an athlete and then move on," said Geoff Hollister, Nike's grass-roots marketing manager, who trained under Bowerman while at the University of Oregon.

Knight, a marketing wiz, was expert at taking Bowerman's solution and making it available to the masses.

But Bowerman was more than an innovative shoe designer. He was one of the greatest track-and-field coaches in the U.S. He coached 24 National Collegiate Athletic Association individual champions, four NCAA team champions, 64 All-Americans and the 1972 Olympic track-and-field team.

In love with running, he wanted others to find the same enjoyment. He started jogging classes and encouraged people of all ages to stay fit through jogging. To interest the public, he wrote the 1967 book *Jogging*, outlining the joys and benefits of the sport. The book helped propel jogging into a national pastime.

Bowerman's actions were "all driven by helping us perform better and to help us reach our maximum," Hollister said.

This drive led Bowerman to experiment and innovate. He helped develop rubberized asphalt runways for track-and-field events, providing a surface that was safer than grass — especially in the rain. He made sure his team wore clothes of the lightest weight possible, including their jerseys. But he really focused on shoes.

"Poorly designed shoes, I felt, caused more shinsplints, foot sores, leg cramps, and aching knees and backs than anything else I knew," he told *Guideposts.*

His aim was to make a lighter running shoe. He figured that for every ounce removed from the shoe's weight, 200 cumulative pounds would be lifted from the runner during a one-mile race. At the time he developed the Waffle sole, his aim was to make a better jogging shoe that was light, had good traction and a clog-resistant pattern.

Bowerman continually pursued excellence. At Nike, "He was very conscious of quality," Knight told *The [Portland] Oregonian,* "and those are things that echo here to this day."

To make sure his guidelines for quality were followed, Bowerman would go over and over them at board meetings.

"It used to irritate me when he would criticize so much," Knight said. "A lot of the times it was a bit of a pain to have a board meeting interrupted by him saying how bad the product was."

But over time, Knight came to believe that Bowerman was Nike's most valuable asset. He stood up for what he believed in, and he believed the company had to keep improving to stay ahead.

Bowerman, whom Knight terms his hero, was a leader and most of all a teacher, Knight says. Bowerman hated to be called coach and insisted his athletes call him Bill. Education was his No. 1 priority and training No. 2.

"The first time I met Bowerman, he conveyed to me he saw himself as an educator on running track and how to go on in life," said Wade Bell, a certified public accountant Bowerman coached from 1964 to 1968. Bell became a half-mile national champion.

Bowerman led by example. He taught his young men and the team at Nike to accept when they were beaten and then pick themselves up again so they could work harder for a better day.

He had an insatiable curiosity and a mind that perceived gaps in the progress of human inventions, J. B. Strasser and Laurie Becklund wrote in *Swoosh: The Unauthorized Story of Nike and the Men Who Played There.*

He had a distinctive way of teaching his team members. He'd use a surplus Army camera to photograph top athletes, mostly in field events. Then he'd loop the film together so that he could show an athlete's technique over and over.

He set up a camera at the finish line and installed a portable darkroom on the field to develop pictures of close finishes.

Bowerman tried to make every athlete feel special. He customized each team member's workout with a strategic plan. He'd sit down with each runner at the beginning of the year and talk about goals, Bell says.

On paper, he'd chart a month-by-month plan, depicting what a runner's time should be at each juncture.

Every Monday, he'd post the workout schedule for each athlete for the week on the locker room door based on those goals, so there was never any confusion about training.

He never let an athlete enter a race without a precise plan on how to run every lap.

Bowerman had runners do test runs to prepare psychologically for a race.

This gave them confidence in their speed and acceleration.

He taught his athletes to assess and reassess every aspect of their performances and those of their competitors, wrote Strasser and Becklund. He'd tell them that every weakness in a competitor could mean an advantage.

"Victory is doing the best you can, and even if you lose, you will have learned something," he said.

He knew how important it was not to spend all one's energy in one place. He insisted his athletes under-train to prevent injuries and reserve strength for meaningful races. His philosophy was to work out hard one day, take a light workout the next day and then push hard again.

Bowerman used visualization to figure out how to attain his goals. Then he'd have his runners and employees do the same.

2

Animator Walt Disney
His Innovation And Persistence
Gave Birth To Magic

Walt Disney was down but not out. It was 1928, and the 26-year-old cartoon animator was taking the train back to California after a disastrous trip to New York City.

His sly distributor had just taken over the rights to Disney's first big-time character, Oswald the Lucky Rabbit, hiring away Disney's best animators in the process.

Although his studio was left unstaffed and in debt, Disney wouldn't admit defeat. Instead, he vowed to start over with what he had — his talent.

As the train shot through the Midwest, Disney started doodling on a piece of paper. It wasn't long before Disney thought the doodles looked like a mouse.

"What do you think of the name Mortimer Mouse?" Disney asked his wife, Lilly.

"Mortimer?" said Lilly, frowning. "How about Mickey?"

Disney (1901–66) had created Mickey Mouse, the most popular cartoon figure in the world, at a time when his future looked its worst.

"Walt never thought he was beaten at anything — ever," said Lilly later, in *The Man Behind the Magic: The Story of Walt Disney*, by Katherine and Richard Greene.

His persistence would lead him to ever-greater achievement in cartoon animation. During his career of more than 40 years, Disney's studios set the standard for animated and family films, winning

48 Academy Awards. His corporate legacy continues as The Walt Disney Co.

A strict, hard-working father and a fun-loving mother gave Disney the early traits he needed.

As a boy, Walt drew whenever he had a chance, and his parents encouraged him. He drew animals on toilet paper and littered the margins of his notebooks with cartoon characters. When the teacher let him, Disney drew on the blackboard and told stories to the class.

While working for the Red Cross Ambulance Corps in World War I in France, Disney practiced his skills by decorating friends' jackets with fake medals and painting helmets to seem more battle-hardened.

A member of Disney's unit, Ray Kroc (later the builder of McDonald's Corp.), recalled that Disney was "regarded as a strange duck, because whenever we had time off and went on the town to chase girls, he stayed in the camp drawing pictures."

The time he spent drawing paid off. He gained confidence through his practice. By the time he returned to the U.S. in 1919, the 18-year-old Disney was ready to open his first commercial art business in Kansas City, Mo.

Disney knew little about business then, however. The studio closed within a year, but it set him on his path.

He took a job as an animator for an early cartoon studio in 1920. All the while, Disney kept looking to make improvements in the way cartoons were filmed. To test his ideas, he persuaded his boss to let him borrow a film camera during his off-hours. Disney took it to his father's garage and tried new techniques such as using drawings for film frames instead of standard paper cutouts.

"Instead of standing back while others experimented," the Greenes wrote, "[Disney's] intuition told him that it was vital to lead the pack."

Opening Disney Bros. Studio with his brother, Roy, in 1923, Walt set a pattern of pushing ahead, even if it meant putting the company's future on the line. As soon as profits came in, Disney spent them on an innovation. First it was adding sound to his cartoons, then adding color.

Then Disney took a huge leap of faith. He knew people loved cartoons. Why not produce a full-length, animated feature?

The idea had distributors worried about leaving successful formulas. Family members worried about gambling away profits. Disney ignored them all. He insisted that if they wanted to get anywhere, they had to go further than they'd already been.

He released *Snow White and the Seven Dwarfs* in 1937. It was an instant hit.

"Here was a cartoon, and here was the audience crying," said Disney animator Ward Kimball in Kathy Merlock Jackson's *Walt Disney: A Bio-Bibliography*. "The biggest stars [attending the premiere], you name them, all crying their eyes out."

Disney took any criticism as a challenge to prove himself right. In 1934, when critics argued that audiences wouldn't sit still for feature-length animation, Disney led some artists to a barely lit stage. Then he single-handedly acted out the plot to *Snow White*, winning over the audience by putting himself completely into each character.

Disney believed that if he made a project as good as he possibly could, people would like it, and the profits would eventually follow.

"If you want to know the real secret of [Disney's] success," Kimball said, "it's that he never tried to make money."

Disney had a vision: an amusement park — Disneyland — where all his ideas and characters could come to life.

In the 1950s, though, amusement-park owners told him he was out of his mind. Disney believed in his idea with steadfast conviction. He borrowed $100,000 against his life insurance, sold his vacation home in Palm Springs, Calif., and started raising money through the *Disneyland* television series on the ABC network.

"I've only thought of money in one way," Disney said, "and that is to do something with. I plow back everything I make into the company. I look at it this way: If I can't use the money now, if I can't have fun with it, I'm not going to be able to take it with me."

Knowing that his work could only improve if he improved himself, "Disney's greatest pleasure was in seeing new things and talking to interesting people," the Greenes said. "Whether he was chatting with a scientist or a street sweeper, he asked question after probing question until he had some idea how they did their jobs. Tooting train whistles made Walt happier than collecting an armful of Oscars."

That kind of curiosity was apparent to anyone who met Disney. Although his grammar, spelling and pronunciation were often poor, many people remarked that Disney was one of the most educated men they ever met.

"Curiosity keeps leading us down new paths," Disney said.

While demanding the best from his employees, Disney tried to understand their viewpoints. When an artist for *Fantasia* complained about working on a scene because he didn't like ballet, Disney gave him season tickets to a famous ballet and sent him backstage to spend time with the dancers. The man discovered he loved ballet and returned to the project.

To forge tighter bonds with workers, Disney insisted they call him by his first name. He dropped past their desks to watch their progress. As long as they produced good work, he'd tolerate almost anything except laziness, dishonesty or a negative attitude.

"If he feels sour," said Disney of one employee, "he shouldn't work here. We are selling happiness."

Aware of the importance of detail, Disney allowed almost six months to finish a three-minute sequence of *Snow White* in which the dwarfs sing "Heigh-Ho" as they travel through the forest. When Disney decided Snow White's cheeks were too pale, he ordered his inkers to go back and add blush to tens of thousands of drawings, even though the film was nearly due in theaters.

"Disney had only one rule," said an animator. "Whatever we did had to be better than anybody else could do it."

3

Media Innovator
Oprah Winfrey

Staying Positive Helped Her
Climb To The Top

Early in the summer of 1993, Oprah Winfrey was in Miami at the annual American Booksellers Association convention.

Alfred A. Knopf was set to publish Winfrey's memoir that fall, and the talk show host was there to press the flesh. She and the publisher pulled out all the stops with a splashy presentation and big party.

Winfrey was the talk of the convention; the book was pronounced a certain bestseller. But just two weeks later, Winfrey decided that the finished product wasn't finished enough. She didn't think the autobiography was her best work. So she pulled it off the publisher's list. It has never been published.

Her action showed two key aspects of her approach to life and business.

First, Winfrey is committed to high quality. If the quality isn't there, "you have the right to change your mind," she said in an interview with the Academy of Achievement shortly after her induction into the organization's Hall of Fame.

Second, Winfrey says, you should go with your gut. "I am where I am today because I allowed myself to listen to my [instincts,]" she said.

She uses that approach when she interviews people. As she told *Cosmopolitan* magazine, she researches her topics and interview subjects carefully. To avoid a canned feel, though, she doesn't often use scripted questions. She prefers the adrenalin of asking "what feels right."

Certainly Winfrey feels right these days. She's the host and owner of *The Oprah Winfrey Show*, which consistently wins high ratings, and the founder of Harpo Productions, which produces her television shows and movies.

She set up a foundation to help underprivileged families get back on their feet and began one of the most influential informal book clubs in the world. Her *O, The Oprah Magazine*, launched by Hearst Publications in 2000, ranked in the top tier of new magazines for circulation and advertising, becoming the first magazine ever to be both *Advertising Age* Launch of the Year and Magazine of the Year. In 2003, Oprah Winfrey became the first African-American woman to join the ranks of billionaires.

Early on, however, Winfrey seemed more like a candidate for welfare rolls than film roles. Born illegitimate to teen-age parents in 1954, she spent her first six years living with her grandparents in her native Kosciusko, Miss. Eventually, she moved in with her mother in Milwaukee.

At age 9 she was raped by an older cousin and was then abused by other relatives during the next several years. Acting out, she became a wild child and got pregnant at 13. Her baby, born prematurely, died shortly after its birth.

Rather than give in to despair and fall further into a life of misery, Oprah refused to give up. She looked at what she'd been through in her young life and decided she'd dedicate herself to changing it.

Life is a marathon, she decided; you don't win or lose at every turn. "I think the ones who survive in life do it by hammering at it one day at a time," she said in Janet Lowe's book, *Oprah Winfrey Speaks*.

Her mother sent her to her father, who was a barber and businessman in Nashville, Tenn. There, she focused on self-improvement.

Vernon Winfrey realized his daughter needed some inspiration. He told her how good she could be and encouraged her lifelong love of books.

He also taught her that to succeed, she always had to pursue excellence. When Vernon set a goal, he focused totally on its achievement. To make sure he'd get there, he'd put in longer hours than anyone else and always tried to do his best. He refused to undercut himself by thinking about failure.

His daughter absorbed that attitude. "There is no such thing as failure in my life," Oprah said. "I just don't believe in it."

Vernon also taught her to reject fear. If she was afraid to try something, he told her, she'd never know whether she could do it, and she'd miss an opportunity.

"The true test of courage," Oprah said, "is to be afraid and to go ahead and do it anyway — to be scared, to have your knees knocking, but to walk on in there anyway."

That's exactly what she did. She told herself that she'd find something she loved to do and then be the best at it. She knew she could present herself well and had a knack for talking with people. She'd been speaking in front of audiences since she was only 4 years old, touring local churches and reciting others' sermons by memory.

She decided to concentrate on what she did best and landed a job as a news reader at a Nashville television station in 1974.

Once there, Winfrey followed her father's example — she put in long hours and prepared carefully before going on camera. She'd bone up on topics she knew she'd be reading about so she'd be ready if something happened to her notes.

Her hard work paid off: She moved up swiftly to news reader and reporter in Baltimore and was offered her own talk show in 1977.

To get interview subjects to open up to her on the show, Winfrey would look for a common bond. She knew she had a winning formula when Baltimore viewers told researchers that what they liked best about her show was how much they learned from it and could apply to their own lives.

Winfrey looked for a bigger market to conquer and decided to go to Chicago in 1984.

Network executives took note of her show's soaring success there and offered her a national spot. In 1986, she began broadcasting nationally. She reaches people all over the world through syndication.

Luck had nothing to do with her success, she thinks.

"I don't believe in luck," she said. "I think luck is preparation meeting opportunity."

When Winfrey doesn't know something, she doesn't try to bluff her way through it. She admits right upfront that she's uninformed and wants to learn about the topic.

Take one of her first assignments as a reporter. She was told to cover a city council meeting — but had no idea how to go about it.

She could try to wing it, but if she missed something important, she'd put her entire career in jeopardy.

She decided to confront the problem head-on and ask others for their help. "I walked into the city council meeting and announced to everybody there, 'This is my first day on the job, and I don't know anything. Please help me.' And they did. . . . Everybody needs someone to show them the way out or up. Everybody."

Winfrey constantly tries to catalog her strengths and weaknesses to find areas she can improve.

"I think the ability to be as good as you can be comes from understanding who you are and what you can and cannot do," she said. "And what you can't do is far more important than what you can do, if what you can't do is going to keep you from flying high."

When she hires people, Winfrey looks for people who can do what she can't.

"I surround myself with people who are smarter than I am," she said. That way, "I feel I can learn something."

4

Industrialist Andrew Carnegie
His Innovations Led The U.S. Into The Steel Age

Fourteen-year-old Andrew Carnegie saw his messenger job at Western Union as one thing — an opportunity to move up. He had a concrete plan too: Do more than was expected, so he'd get noticed by his bosses.

He started by memorizing names, addresses and faces of people to whom he made frequent deliveries. Soon he recognized many of them on the street and cut his delivery time. Then he taught himself to operate the telegraph.

His plan worked. Shortly thereafter, he was promoted to telegraph operator.

"The battle of life is already half won by the young man who is brought personally in contact with high officials," Carnegie said. "Everybody should do something beyond the sphere of his duties — something [that] attracts the attention of those over him."

Carnegie (1835–1919) went on to found Carnegie Steel Co. and become one of the richest men in the world. The manufacturing innovations he introduced lowered the price of steel, affecting virtually every aspect of life — from machinery (and productivity) to skyscrapers and low-cost housing, historian Paul Johnson wrote in the July 1999 issue of *Commentary* magazine.

"By achieving economies of scale, [he] turned the luxuries of the rich into the necessities of the poor and thereby reduced the real price of almost everything," Johnson wrote.

Carnegie was born in Dunfermline, Scotland. His father was a weaver who lost his job when the looms were automated. The family moved to Pittsburgh in 1848.

Young Andrew, just 12 at the time and with only five years of schooling behind him, went to work as a bobbin boy in a textile mill and then in a factory tending a steam engine and boiler. Each time, he tried to do his best and then some. In late 1849 he joined Western Union.

In 1853 he took a position as personal telegrapher and assistant to Thomas Scott, an executive with the Pennsylvania Railroad. To make sure he understood everything that happened around him, Carnegie studied the railroad's operations in depth.

He became so knowledgeable about them that he often suggested innovations. For example, he proposed that the railroad burn cars after accidents rather than try to remove them from the tracks. His suggestion cleared the tracks more quickly.

Not surprisingly, when Scott was promoted in 1859, Carnegie jumped at the chance to take his place as superintendent of the Pennsylvania Railroad's Western Division. By then, though, Carnegie could've supported himself from his investments.

He'd always been careful with money. "Take care of the pennies, and the pounds will take care of themselves" was a motto he lived by. Even when he earned just $2 or $3 a week, he'd put a little aside. In 1856, he invested his savings and a small bank loan in the Woodruff Sleeping Car Co., which shortly began returning $5,000 a year to him — double his annual railroad salary.

After several other successful investments (including one in the first major oil strike in the U.S. at Titusville, Pa.), Carnegie decided he wanted to sink his money into something he'd build. He quit the railroad in 1865 and helped found the Keystone Bridge Co. to replace wooden bridges with iron.

Then, in 1872, he saw Henry Bessemer's blast furnaces during a visit to England. The steel that Bessemer's new process could forge inspired Carnegie. He immediately saw the possibilities of steel as a structural material because of its strength and flexibility.

He returned to the U.S. and planned his first steel mill in the business that was to become Carnegie Steel. To gain attention for the new business, he deployed a clever marketing strategy: He named the plant the Edgar Thomson Works after the president of the Pennsylvania Railroad.

Not surprisingly, Carnegie's first order was for 2,000 steel rails — from the Pennsylvania Railroad.

Although his business was successful from the beginning, Carnegie knew he couldn't keep up the pace or the quality all by himself, wrote Julie M. Fenster in her book, *In the Words of Great Business Leaders*. "He admitted that he had 'no shadow of a claim to a rank as inventor, chemist, investigator or mechanician,'" Fenster wrote.

He hired those who did. He hired a chemist to find out exactly what happened inside his furnaces and to ensure that they operated at maximum efficiency. (He was one of the first industrialists to use scientists to research his own business.) He hired top accountants who instituted strict cost-accounting measures.

As a result, he reduced the cost of rails from $160 a ton in 1875 to $17 by 1890.

Once he hired people, Carnegie didn't micromanage. According to Fenster, Carnegie believed that "a good executive did not hold the reins of day-to-day management. His job was to implement a progressive system, install worthy employees and chart an accurate course. If he had to watch over the employees to get the best out of them, then they were flawed and so was the system."

That isn't to say Carnegie kept his hands off the business; instead, he chose his moments to get involved.

For example, "If you want [to win] a contract," Carnegie said, "be on the spot when it is let." He believed that unforeseen circumstances could come up after bids were submitted and that being on hand at the letting could make the difference between winning and losing a contract.

In fact, he added, whenever possible, "stay on hand until you can take the written contract home in your pocket."

Carnegie ensured that when a company dealt with Carnegie Steel, they got a high-quality product. "Subject all products to more rigid tests than the purchaser requires," he said. "A reputation for producing the best is a sure foundation on which to build."

To keep his perspective fresh, Carnegie spent as much time as possible out of the office, Fenster says. He took up to six months a year traveling in Europe. "He did not want to allow his mind to carve itself into a rut," Fenster said.

That fresh viewpoint might have given him the strength to swim against the economic currents.

"Carnegie Steel always expanded during panics or depressions," Fenster wrote. Even as stock prices fell, taking the market for metals with them, "Carnegie would put every penny he could into building up his facilities."

Carnegie believed in doing one thing and doing it well. When he expanded, he didn't go into collateral businesses but expanded steel production or bought coal, coke mines and ships to transport raw materials to — and finished goods from — his plants.

"Put your eggs in one basket," he said, "and watch the basket. That's how to make money." He disdained executives who invested in "faraway enterprises" rather than modernizing their own factories.

If Carnegie's well known for what he built, he's equally renowned for what he gave away. He believed the wealthy had a moral obligation to act as stewards for society. "The man who dies rich dies disgraced," he said.

In 1901, he sold Carnegie Steel to J. P. Morgan for $480 million. Before Carnegie died in 1919, he gave approximately 90% of that away, establishing foundations or distributing it himself.

5

Publisher Katharine Graham
She Built Her Career On Persistence
And Integrity

Katharine Graham (1917–2001) transformed herself from a shy woman of privilege into one of America's most powerful publishers by calling on her inner strength and steely resolve.

The former publisher of the *Washington Post* and chief executive and chairman of The Washington Post Co. was a blend of gutsy leadership, journalistic integrity and caring. The combination proved crucial in turning the *Post* from a media also-ran into one of the nation's most powerful and must-read dailies.

She faced problems with calm and courage. "She found she could seize the moment and rise to the challenge, and she did," Jack Valenti said in a 2001 interview. Valenti, head of the Motion Picture Association of America, was a longtime Graham friend.

Valenti says he first encountered her steely character when he served as a special assistant to President Lyndon Johnson and Graham was the *Post*'s publisher. A sometimes-angry LBJ would storm into his White House office telling Valenti to get Graham on the phone to protest a story from that morning's *Post*.

"Well, she always received it graciously, but she never backed off," Valenti said. "LBJ said to me one time, 'By God, she doesn't cut and run for the people that work for her!' LBJ understood that, even though he used to get purple with rage over some of the stories. She was extraordinary."

Graham knew how important good communication is and worked continually to keep the lines open. To keep from being

blindsided by a story, for example, Graham created the "no surprise" rule with *Post* managing editor Ben Bradlee. "I didn't want
to read anything in the paper of great importance or that represented an abrupt change which we hadn't discussed; that I wanted
to be in on the takeoffs as well as the landings," Graham wrote in
her memoir, *Personal History*, for which she won a 1998 Pulitzer
Prize. "I expected to have a 'constant conversation' in which we
would each know what the other was thinking."

She didn't shy from making tough decisions. When the *Post* got
hold of then-Defense Secretary Robert McNamara's classified 47-vol-
ume history of U.S. involvement in Indochina — the Pentagon
Papers — Graham was the pivotal decision maker. She was under
tremendous pressure not to publish. The *New York Times*, which
had already published its first installments of the papers, was under
court injunction to stop further publication. Then there was the issue
of the Post Co.'s upcoming public stock offering. The company
would now be financially vulnerable.

"Frightened and tense, I took a big gulp and said, 'Go ahead, go
ahead, go ahead. Let's go. Let's publish,' " Graham wrote.

It was a momentous journalistic decision and, according to
Bradlee's memoir, *A Good Life*, reflected the new level of self-confidence Graham's leadership had helped usher in.

Shortly thereafter, the case was decided in favor of the *Post* and
the *New York Times* by a 6–3 Supreme Court decision.

"The material in the Pentagon Papers was just the kind of information the public needed in order to form its opinions and make its
choices more wisely," Graham wrote.

As committed as she was to the public's right to know, Graham
was keenly aware of the need for balance. During the heat of the
paper's coverage to expose the Watergate cover-up of the break-in at
the Democratic Headquarters, Graham demanded her staff's coverage be fair and even-keeled.

Rick Smith, chairman and editor in chief of *Newsweek*, says
Graham constantly asked tough questions: Did they get it right?
Were they fair? How could they have done it better?

"Those simple questions — repeated over and over, whether
there was any public outcry or not — might seem quaintly old-fash-
ioned in an age of spin," Smith wrote in the *Post*. "But it was pre-
cisely that kind of integrity, that restlessness to do things better, to

try to 'get it right,' that made Kay a beacon to all who cared about the values of our craft."

That approach earned the *Post* a Pulitzer Prize and helped bring about the resignation of President Richard Nixon in 1974.

Graham's operating principle was that good journalism is good business. "We operated under the philosophy — which I have espoused and practiced from the time I took over the company — that journalistic excellence and profitability go hand in hand."

"She had a resolve and a persistence, I guess the word is fiduciary, not in a financial sense but in the sense that she had a responsibility with this newspaper," Valenti said.

Graham absorbed that attitude from her father, Eugene Meyer. He'd made a fortune on Wall Street and bought a bankrupt *Washington Post* in 1933 after offering a bid of $825,000 at a public auction. With a circulation of 50,000, the paper was losing $1 million a year. Meyer was sure he could meet the challenge.

His daughter believed she could, too. At the University of Chicago, where she'd earn a bachelor's degree in American history that meant enrolling in Mortimer Adler's legendary "Great Books" course. In these seminars, Graham learned how to verbally thrust and parry.

"The methods they used often taught you most about standing up, about challenging them and fundamentally pleasing [the teachers] by doing it with gusto and verve, so that they were amused," Graham wrote.

After a move back to Washington, D.C., she got a job editing the *Post*'s letters to the editor section. She married Phil Graham. Her father soon enjoined Phil to become the *Post*'s publisher, a job he took in 1946.

But the death of her father and suicide of her husband forced Graham into new paths. The shy young woman suddenly found herself the new president of The Washington Post Co. in 1963.

Graham decided on a learn-by-doing approach to understand how the *Post*, *Newsweek* and the Post Co.'s television stations all worked. She asked everyone questions. She called in reporters and talked to them about their stories to learn about the issues and her workers. She let her team know she was behind them — flying to New York City every Monday and Tuesday to personally attend *Newsweek*'s editorial meeting and cover story conferences.

Despite the challenge — "I am quaking in my boots a little," she wrote a friend — Graham faced down her fears. She pushed herself to keep moving and position the *Post* for new heights.

"I had come to realize that I could only do the job in whatever way I could do it," Graham said. "I couldn't try to be someone else."

That realization proved to be the key to the paper's and her own future success.

6

Applied Materials' James Morgan

Listening To Employees Kept His Company Growing

James Morgan learned his first business secret as a 15-year-old overseeing 35 farm workers at his family's cannery: Invest in your people, teach them, support them, and they'll take you to the top.

When employees were paid well, they stayed loyal. When they were shown respect, they responded in kind. When they learned new techniques at work, they used them to increase business.

That same simple approach permeated Morgan's leadership strategy as chief executive of Santa Clara, Calif.–based Applied Materials Inc. The company's thousands of employees make the machines that stamp out microchips for the Internet, personal computers and cell phones.

"Helping people in organizations meet their potential is my primary personal motivation in business," said the company leader, who announced his retirement in April 2003.

Morgan's 27 years at Applied Materials' helm — the longest tenure of any major tech CEO — saw the company's value increase 4,456.5 times, from $5.4 million to $24.2 billion, according to *Fortune* magazine. Morgan will stay on as Applied Materials' chairman of the board.

Behind Morgan's desk hangs a poster that says, "Press on: Nothing in the world can take the place of persistence." Morgan made sure each senior manager had a copy.

He tries to stay on top of trends in the marketplace, and he's done so consistently before his competitors.

After he came on as CEO in 1977, at age 38, Morgan's keen eye led him to invest heavily in Japan and other Asian countries just before they shot to prominence. He ignored those who said he was off the mark. As of 2000, Applied Materials earned half its revenue from Asia.

During periods of recession in the 1980s, Morgan swam against the current and poured investment dollars into research and development.

Such moves have earned him a giant's reputation in the Silicon Valley.

"He's one of the best managers in America," said Dan Hutcheson, a research analyst with VLSI Research Inc. in San Jose, Calif., who's followed Applied Materials and the semiconductor industry for more than 20 years.

With Morgan at the helm, Applied Materials became the world's leading semiconductor equipment manufacturer in 1992, passing the billion-dollar-revenue mark the following year. Revenue increased from $3 billion in 1995 to $4.8 billion in 1999.

Morgan's astute management, combined with the ever-increasing global appetite for microchips, promised a winning combination. Applied Materials' customers include Intel Corp., Lucent Technologies and Motorola Corp.

That the same chief executive could keep a company in renewal and flourishing for so many years is a credit to his ability to change.

"Very few leaders can grow from being a sub-$100 million company to $100 million to $1 billion-plus," Hutcheson said. "That's a rare commodity. Most companies replace their management several times along that path. It takes a different mind-set. You really have to transform yourself to make those kinds of jumps."

But Morgan's management philosophy includes fresh approaches. To counter cubicle myopia and keep everyone thinking, he asks employees to spend 5% of their workday "envisioning the future." Workers are expected to have three things they're "thinking about" but not yet "taking action on."

"Individuals in organizations get into a very reactive mode," Morgan said. "What we try to do is get [employees] to spend some of their time thinking about what might happen, therefore begin to anticipate and therefore [be] in a position to be prepared for change."

Morgan keeps in touch with this fresh thinking by what he calls "porpoising" through the company. Before he makes a key decision, he dives through various levels of the organization, getting input and feedback from low-, mid- and upper-level workers.

When a bottleneck developed a few years ago that threatened the manufacturing-to-marketplace rhythm, Morgan had an answer. After products were developed by engineering and thrown over to manufacturing and marketing, they were dying there.

According to Hutcheson, "Morgan solved the problem by giving the engineer a share in the success of the product. [Now the engineer] made sure the product worked when it got to the field. The bugs were fixed and fixed fast."

Morgan stays down to earth. He lunches in the employee cafeteria. He requested more than $25,000 in pay cuts in 2001 and asked that his bonus ($3 million in 2000) be withheld in 2001 and 2002 because of the company's lowered performance in the economic downturn. He has the same office he started with — an unpretentious room in the manufacturing building. And he's been married to the same woman since 1960.

But he understands how to keep everyone on his toes. One way is to hire a few more managers than he really needs. That way, "Everyone knows they have to compete to keep their position," Hutcheson said. "The people on the team know that if they don't perform, there is always someone right behind them ready to take their slot."

It was as a teen-ager on the family farm in Indiana that Morgan decided he wanted to lead a company. He played basketball at Mercersburg Academy in Pennsylvania, where he learned teamwork and court smarts, qualities that made Indiana hero Larry Bird synonymous with a team approach to getting things done. Said Morgan: "You really had to be collectively successful."

At Cornell University, Morgan took a five-year program that earned him a bachelor's in mechanical engineering in 1962 and an MBA in 1963. But it was in the Reserve Officers' Training Corps that he learned some of his most valuable skills. He added that he incorporated ROTC leadership principles — taking responsibility for those under one's charge, setting the example — into his company training.

After Cornell, Morgan served as a management consultant in the U.S. Army Materiel Command from 1963 to 1965 examining corporate management techniques and production technologies and reporting them to the Army.

Morgan constantly tried to learn from the techniques he came across. He learned so much after studying management decentralization at industrial conglomerate Textron Inc. that when he left the Army, Textron hired the 29-year-old to run a division of 1,600 employees based in the San Francisco Bay area. Morgan spent four years there gaining what he calls "good turnaround experience."

"[Textron was] losing about $15 million on this sophisticated government contract. They couldn't perform technically. We were about a year behind schedule. Other than that, it was in good shape," Morgan said, laughing.

After getting the Textron unit afloat, Morgan left and joined WestVen, a venture capital firm where he used his management experience to select investments and advise new companies. But his ambition nagged at him. When the top job at Applied Materials came up, Morgan leapt at the chance.

He started as chief executive in 1977. His first directive, after a thorough review, was to pare down the company to doing what it did best and sticking with that.

He stripped away five of six divisions. He jettisoned wafer-cleaning equipment and solid-state power supplies. The company's focus became making machines that make microchips.

The first few months proved a financial bungee jump. "It was a $29 million [company], and I took it down to $14 million," Morgan said. "That was tough. [At] one of my first all-employee meetings I said: 'You lost sight of some basics. We need to lead from our strengths [and] concentrate our resources.' I bring that out every now and then to our people because they forget that sometimes."

To make sure his message got across, Morgan walked the floors of the company and told everyone about it personally.

The employees listened. The company pulled out of a nosedive and won a success beyond that envisioned by his board. For his leadership and vision, Morgan received the National Medal of Technology in 1996.

7

Hewlett-Packard's
Carly Fiorina

How A Philosophy Major Came To
Drive Technology's Big Engines

D on't go, friends and colleagues warned. It was 1989, and Carly Fiorina, then 35, was weighing a division transfer at AT&T Corp. from communications services to the Network Systems Division.

It would be a lousy career move, most fellow workers said. Network Systems, the forerunner of Lucent Technologies Corp., was a technology-driven division controlled by engineers. While Fiorina could boast a degree from Stanford University, her studies were in philosophy and medieval history — not engineering.

To make matters worse, the culture at Network Systems was "traditional, hierarchical and male dominated," Fiorina recalled in a 1999 interview. So was the Asian market, where she'd be expected to negotiate joint ventures on Network Systems' behalf. Her work in the communications division was far easier: selling long-distance time to the federal government.

But Fiorina had an appetite for risk and felt that "change is always more interesting to me than momentum." As for education, she thought her liberal arts background would give her "a broad perspective on the world and on life — an important element in any kind of success," she said.

She was right. Fiorina held several executive positions at Network Systems and Lucent Technologies Corp. before becoming president and CEO of computer giant Hewlett-Packard in 1999.

From 1997 to 1999, Fiorina served as group president of Lucent's Global Service Provider business, which sold and provided network systems and software for telephone, Internet and wireless service providers. In 1998, her group accounted for $19 billion in sales, or 58% of total revenue from continuing operations at Lucent, North America's largest maker of communications gear.

Just Say Yes

Fiorina has been ignoring the naysayers ever since the seventh grade, when she decided to study classical languages and read Aristotle in the original Greek. "People told me it's too hard, you can't do that, but I did it anyway," she said.

Born in Austin, Texas, Fiorina attended high schools in Ghana, London, North Carolina and Palo Alto, Calif. Her abstract-artist mother and law-professor father had an approach to child-rearing that was both liberating and demanding.

On the one hand, Fiorina grew up without a sense of limitations. Despite her sex, she could be or do anything she wanted. On the other hand, her parents had exceedingly high expectations for their daughter, so she didn't want to disappoint them.

But her road to success was hardly the straight course one might expect. She took her time finding what best suited her talents. To be successful, "You have to love what you do, which means you need to know yourself pretty well," Fiorina said.

She attended law school at the University of California, Los Angeles, but dropped out after learning that law "was all about discovering precedent someone else has set. And that didn't strike me as very interesting."

After that, she floated for a while — teaching English in Bologna, Italy, and then working as a receptionist at a commercial brokerage firm. Between phone calls, she began writing deals for brokers, and that's when the light bulb went on.

"I found out I was good at business," Fiorina said. "It was intellectually stimulating, I liked the pace, and I liked the interaction with people."

She went back to school and earned an MBA in marketing from the University of Maryland. Her first job was as a sales rep at

AT&T. When Ma Bell began restructuring operations not too much later, it opened the door to opportunities for adventurous employees like Fiorina.

She quickly advanced to management. Key to her promotions, she says, was staying targeted on the task at hand.

"My advice is to focus 100% on doing the job you have better than anybody else," she said. "I've seen a lot of highflying people fall flat because they were so focused on the next job they didn't get the current job done. Management sees performance as a measure of potential, not potential as a measure of performance."

Fiorina's performance lived up to its potential. In 1995, AT&T chose Fiorina to manage the spinoff of Lucent. The new company had a highly successful $3 billion initial public offering.

She relied on her training in philosophy to anchor her decisions. When she was named to head Lucent's consumer-products division in 1997, she quickly concluded that the group didn't fit with the corporation's business-to-business strategy. Logic dictated she eliminate her own position and sell off most of the division. So she did.

Staying on top of technology is a huge challenge, says Fiorina, who was responsible for products ranging from communications software to routing switches.

At Lucent, she routinely digested written summaries from staff members. Occasionally, she went to a particular person or organization within Lucent and implored, "Teach me about this."

Apt Pupil

When Lucent began a major thrust into optical networking, for instance, she sat down for a two-hour tutorial with Harry Bosco, chief operating officer of Lucent's Optical Networking Group.

But this learning cut both ways. For scientists, explaining the technology to Fiorina sometimes became an exercise in learning how to talk to customers. Fiorina became a stand-in for the end user. "It helps us develop the marketing pitch," she said.

Her input on what her markets need was key to product development.

To decide how the Global Service Provider unit should allocate research and development dollars, Fiorina met regularly with Arun

Netravali, executive vice president of research at Bell Labs, a division of Lucent.

During these dialogues, "He educates me about the technology, and I educate him as to the real application of this technology, the so-what from a business point of view," she said in 1999.

She made it a point never to debate with Netravali about what might be technically feasible to make within a set time. As a non-technical person in a technical environment, "It's important to know what I don't know," Fiorina said.

Fiorina often called on other Lucent executives when evaluating potential employees for her unit.

"I don't think I've ever hired anyone in my career without asking for other input," she said. Even when the interviewers don't see eye-to-eye, "you end up getting additional perspective on someone's capabilities," she said. The new hire "gets an instant network of coaches and supporters."

Bold Move

When Hewlett-Packard tapped Fiorina in 1999 as its first CEO ever pulled from outside HP's ranks, her task was to breath new life into the 60-year-old company. The sluggish economy of the early 2000s toughened that challenge, but Fiorina managed to achieve her biggest goal so far: the $18.7 billion acquisition/merger with computer maker Compaq in May 2002.

Though highly criticized, both inside and out of HP — she barely won shareholder approval and faced a court challenge and strong opposition led by co-founder Hewlett's son — Fiorina's bold move helped the company retake the No. 1 spot in global PC market share from Dell Computers in the fourth quarter of 2002.

When Fiorina left Lucent to head up Hewlett-Packard in 1999, she became the first woman to run a Dow 30 company. She was named the most powerful woman in American business by *Forbes* magazine five years in a row (1998–2002).

8

Cosmetics Queen
Mary Kay Ash
She Made Beauty A Big Seller

It wasn't worrying about what went wrong, thought Mary Kay Ash (1915–2001); it was all about focusing on what was going right.

She'd retired in 1963 after spending 25 years working for several companies in direct sales. As she wrote in her autobiography, while she loved the work, she didn't like the attitude: "There were times when I would be asked to take a man out on the road to train him, and for six months of training he would be brought back to Dallas, made my superior and given twice my salary! It happened more than once."

She found herself bitter. As Ash wrote in *On People Management*, another of her books: "To ward off those feelings, I decided to make a list of only those good things that had happened to me during the previous 25 years. Forcing myself to think positively did wonders for my spirit."

At first, she thought the list she'd compiled might become the basis for a book, one that could help other women in the same predicament. But somewhere along the line, she asked herself: "Why write about a company based on Golden Rule management techniques? Instead of just writing about it, why not give it a try myself?"

Do It Yourself

She'd recently purchased the rights to a series of skin-care products originally developed by a tanner who discovered that the solutions he worked with in leather kept the skin of his hands youthful looking. He modified the solutions for use on the face as well as hands.

"I knew that these skin-care products were tremendous, and with some modifications and high-quality packaging, I was sure they would be big sellers," Ash wrote.

She financed the company with her life savings of $5,000, and on Sept. 13, 1963, opened Mary Kay Cosmetics in a 500-square-foot Dallas storefront and plowed ahead, using the grit and determination instilled in her during a difficult childhood.

Mary Kathleen Wagner had a difficult childhood. At age 6, she had to take care of an ill father while her mother worked two jobs. She still did well in school and found time to participate in extracurricular activities. "My mother's words became the theme of my childhood," Ash said. "They have stayed with me all my life: 'You can do it.'"

While Ash had no experience running a company, she'd worked with people she felt couldn't manage either. She planned to learn from those negative experiences.

For example, she remembered once waiting in a long line to meet a sales manager who'd delivered an inspiring speech earlier in the day. She waited three hours, but when it was her turn: "He never even looked at me. Instead he looked over my shoulder to see how much longer the line was. Right on the spot I made a decision that if I ever became someone people waited in line to shake hands with, I'd give the person my undivided attention — no matter how tired I was."

She made a point of knowing all her employees until that became physically impossible. But even as the company grew from its initial nine employees to more than 850,000 with $1 billion in sales, she'd send each employee a personal birthday card.

Ash set high standards for her employees. "My experience with people is that they generally do what you expect them to!" she wrote. "If you expect them to perform well, they will; conversely, if you expect them to perform poorly, they'll probably oblige. I believe that average employees who try their hardest to live up to your high expectations of them will do better than above-average people with low self-esteem."

She felt it important, too, that supervisors let employees know that their work is appreciated. "I never yet met a person who didn't want to be appreciated," Ash wrote. At Mary Kay, Ash set up a thank-you system that ranges from a simple "thank you for showing up early" to a pink Cadillac.

The company is well known for giving the expensive luxury car to its top producers. Ash said the vehicles were chosen because of their association with excellence.

Whatever incentive program the company runs, Ash wrote: "We go first class, and although it's expensive, it's worth it, because our people are made to feel important. . . . It [is] our way of telling our people how important they are to our company. . . . We might settle for one elegant banquet a year rather than two moderate ones."

Ash thought that one of her most important management tools was her ability to listen. She called it "the most undervalued of communication skills" and suggested "that's why God gave us two ears and only one mouth."

Make It Personal

Beyond listening, Ash said, it's important to solicit opinions. One of the best managers she ever worked for always asked, "What do you think you should do?"

Asking for employee opinions makes them feel important. Just as important, Ash said, it makes them buy into a plan. "People will support that which they help create. When you dictate even the most thoughtful and logical concept to a person — this idea is still a command. When you ask her to contribute to its inception, that very same idea becomes a 'personal crusade.'"

Ash wrote that once she promised something, she had to deliver. "A manager should never make a promise that something will be done unless he is absolutely certain that it will be done! A broken promise is devastating for those who have been disappointed, and there is no excuse for it in management. Furthermore, a manager should never make a commitment unless he has the complete authority to do so."

Ash considered her employees investments and assets. "If we spend six months training someone, only to see that person leave us, we feel we have lost a lot of time and money. So once people come aboard, we make every attempt to keep them. If by chance they don't seem to be working out in one area, we'll try our best to find another spot for them."

Ash once had a secretary who wasn't right for her job. She was conscientious, but something was out of whack. After sitting down and discussing the situation with her, Ash transferred the woman to the accounting department, "where she did a first-rate job. Good people are hard to find — so when you do find them it's important you make every effort to keep them."

9

Self-Help Pioneer
Dale Carnegie
He Won Friends And Influenced
Many People

If ever there were a sad sack who needed the keep-your-chin-up advice of Dale Carnegie (1888–1955), it was Dale Carnegie.

Until he published *How to Win Friends and Influence People* in 1936, the founding guru of the self-help movement had failed at almost everything he'd ever tried, professionally and personally.

He never graduated from college. He tried careers in farming, teaching, salesmanship, acting, journalism and novel writing; all flopped. His first marriage ended in a bitter divorce. He lost most of his savings in the stock market crash of 1929.

His failures often left him depressed. Once he was even suicidal. But his failures made him fascinated with successful people. What exactly did they do? What were their methods?

Carnegie decided it was simple self-confidence. All it needed was to be built up and constantly reinforced.

He studied the subject for years and later compiled his observations into his classic book about speaking and interacting with people.

That wasn't easy for him, either. Carnegie was an intensely shy man who never completely overcame his own fear of public speaking.

Yet an estimated 50 million copies of his books have been sold in dozens of languages. His training courses continue to thrive nationwide, having taught more than 7 million people.

Success at self-help was something he had to work at hard and learn as much as anyone else.

Great Role Models

So he looked to those he most admired. His most famous books rely on quotations from and stories about Abe Lincoln, Benjamin Franklin and other wise figures.

"I realize now that healthy people don't write books on health. It is the sick person who becomes interested in health. And in the same way, people who have a natural gift for diplomacy don't write books on *How to Win Friends and Influence People.* The reason I wrote the book was because I have blundered so often myself, that I began to study the subject for the good of my soul," Carnegie said in 1937.

At least 15 million copies of the book have been sold since then, making it one of the most purchased books of the 20th century.

Carnegie was born in rural Missouri. His real name was Dale Carnagey. Despite rumors, he wasn't related to steel magnate Andrew Carnegie.

He grew up in grinding poverty. He was painfully shy because of his shabby clothes and down-home ways.

"I worried for fear girls would laugh at me if I tipped my hat to them," he wrote in *How to Stop Worrying and Start Living*, his other bestseller.

The turning point in his life came when Carnegie encountered the Chautauqua movement. It was a late 19th century religious movement that prompted spiritual health through adult education.

Carnegie noticed the ability of the Chautauqua lecturers to enthrall crowds with their strong words. Carnegie began practicing, lecturing the livestock in his father's barn for hours on the subjects of the day.

To test his public mettle, he then entered debate contests in school. The first time out, he lost. He lost the second time, too, and several other attempts after that.

But he kept trying, and after several attempts, he won. Other victories followed, and soon he built up enough confidence to hold forth on any topic.

Confronting Fears

Carnegie's experience taught him that the only way to overcome fears was to confront them and not be discouraged by initial failures.

It was a lesson he needed.

Carnegie's first jobs were as a traveling salesman. He sold everything from correspondence courses to hog lard. It was hard work, the hardest part being interacting with people and convincing them to buy his stuff. Those who could interact well succeeded more often than not, he noted.

It was the same thing with his brief acting career. Every night, he had to give the same performance to a new bunch of strangers — and make it convincing. Journalism and novel writing were similar — above all, he had to make his audience interested in what he had to say.

That can't be done if the person trying to do the convincing doesn't believe what he's saying. Self-confidence, he reasoned, was the key not just in these pursuits but also in everything else.

Eventually, he got a job at the YMCA teaching the one thing he knew he could do: public speaking.

The YMCA was hesitant about giving him the job. It didn't think Carnegie's course was worth the $2-a-night salary he requested. To persuade YMCA officials, he struck a deal to work on commission. Soon he was pulling in $30 a night.

The essence of Carnegie's job was getting his students to confront their fears of public speaking. Night after night, he simply made his students talk.

"The way to develop self-confidence, he said, is to do the thing you fear to do and get a record of successful experiences behind you," wrote Lowell Thomas, a friend of Carnegie's, in the original introduction of *How to Win Friends and Influence People*.

Carnegie's books evolved from the speaking courses he taught. He collected the tales, anecdotes and aphorisms he used in a single volume. He wrote them in part because there were no other books he could rely on.

10

NBA Commissioner David Stern

He Pumped Up League Into An Entertainment Powerhouse

In a business where statistics rule supreme, David Stern's are Jordanesque.

When Stern took over as commissioner of the National Basketball Association in 1984, game attendance averaged just 51% of capacity. By 1999, with most teams in newer and larger arenas, NBA attendance stood at 91% of capacity.

In 1984, television income was negligible. The 1999 season was the first year of a four-year contract worth $2.6 billion for domestic television rights alone. Broadcasts in foreign countries of NBA games were shown in 199 nations as the 20th century closed — bringing in additional revenue, but the NBA won't say how much. In 1984, retail sales of NBA-licensed merchandise were $44 million. By 1999, they'd rocketed to about $3 billion a year.

Much of Stern's success comes from his recognition that the NBA could become far more than an association of professional basketball teams. It could become an entertainment and licensing powerhouse. Looking for a model in that arena, he studied the best: Walt Disney Co.

He also recognized that NBA fortunes would rest on the league's image. So he studied branding techniques, again turning to the best. He cut deals to associate the NBA brand with such winners as Coca-Cola, IBM and McDonald's.

Doing It Himself

He closely managed the NBA's public transformation. "No one is going to care about your product as much as you do," he's said.

When Stern made branding a priority, all other factors became secondary, including budgets. Whenever and wherever the league has a special event, Stern says he freely spends "enormous amounts of money" to guarantee it meets sponsor and customer expectations.

Stern said, "We send enormous groups of people to these events," which take place worldwide. They range from the All-Star Weekend to season openers in Japan to the annual McDonald's World Championships in Paris.

Stern's theory: "Every time we have an event, it defines our brand," and to cheapen it to save a few thousand dollars is short-term thinking and ultimately "diminishes its value."

As sellout crowds at the Japan and Paris events indicate, Stern has successfully managed the league's global expansion. While it's unlikely that there will be franchises outside of North America in the foreseeable future, it's hard to travel anywhere in the world today and not run into someone wearing an NBA star's jersey.

This expansion has been fueled by Stern's philosophy — think globally, act locally. Although he's marketing an American-born sport, he understands that selling techniques are particular to every culture.

Operating as the head of a multinational corporation would do, he has NBA employees "on the ground, so that they can be part of the local scene and understand local television sponsorship, local licensing and retailing."

To that end, the NBA has opened offices in London; Paris; Barcelona, Spain; Munich, Germany; Hong Kong; Taipei, Taiwan; Tokyo; Melbourne, Australia and Miami.

Stern, born in 1942, learned the rudiments of business as a boy by working in his father's Manhattan delicatessen. He learned to put in long hours and to wear lots of hats.

"I was an expert at using a mop, as well as doing the counter service and cooking," he said. But the most important thing he learned "is taking care of the customer," from getting orders out quickly to making sure the coffee is steaming.

Even today, while managing a global empire, Stern doesn't let himself lose sight of the details.

Lore has it that once, while attending a buffet for an all-star event, Stern noticed that it was taking people too long to get their food. According to the story, the deli-waiter-turned-commissioner called over one of the caterers and showed him how to speed things up.

Asked whether the story was true, Stern replied: "Yeah, probably. We're defined by how we treat our guests."

In fact, Stern treats everyone well. Gary Bettman, who worked for Stern and is now commissioner of the National Hockey League, says Stern's greatest strength is his ability to bring out the best in people.

He does that by focusing on what's in their best interest. Take how he's united the 29 corporate and individual owners of league teams. Before Stern became commissioner, owners had spent considerable energy bickering among themselves.

He got them to think in terms of the league, by convincing them "that the value of their franchise is completely intertwined with the value of the league as a whole." When making a case to the owners, he always backs it with hard numbers. "We present data to them, and they make action decisions," Stern said.

He's even won the grudging respect of players by persuading them that they, too, have what he calls "a commonality of interest" with the owners. It was this sense of shared interest that led to the players union accepting one of the toughest anti-drug policies in professional sports.

Moreover, players have come to realize that because their salaries are tied to revenue, the more the league earns, the more they do.

Power Of Unity

Getting the owners and players on the same side was a priority from the start, Stern notes. When he set about redefining the NBA as an entertainment and licensing operation — his single most important move in reviving the league — he needed the league's full backing.

But even more important than assuring cooperation has been ensuring the league's fundamental financial soundness. Again looking at league interests as a whole, Stern locked out players in the summer of 1998. For a variety of reasons, including loopholes in free-agency rules, salaries were rising faster than revenue.

"The system needed to be modified, and we felt it was going to be worth the one-time costs," Stern said.

The lockout lasted six months. It cost players an estimated $50 million a week for the 20 lost weeks of the season. Owners and the league lost an additional $25 million to $37 million for each week of the schedule that wasn't played. But Stern wouldn't back away from his priority of making sure NBA teams were on solid footing.

Observers say he achieved his ends.

Stern's ability to see the big picture helps him in staffing, as well. Because he makes certain to hire the right people, he can give employees a lot of autonomy and remain confident the details will be taken care of.

Although Stern has carefully guided the NBA's transformation, he gives his people leeway to implement their own ideas, even when he's not keen on them.

For example, he initially opposed the idea of adding the three-point shooting contest to the NBA All-Star Weekend. But one of his executives was strongly in favor of it. "Go ahead; do it," Stern told the official. It turned out to be one of the weekend's most popular features.

Just as Stern has borrowed heavily from corporate America on how to manage a global brand, he gleefully admits he's willing to copy what works in other sports.

The Legends Game, in which retired hoopsters play during All-Star Weekend, is modeled after Major League Baseball clubs' old-timers games. The dunking contests started in the American Basketball Association. Special parties thrown by sponsors were something he saw at the Olympics and at the Super Bowl.

"If it's a good idea, I'm willing to try it. It doesn't make a difference who invented it," he said.

PART 2

Growing From The Ground Up

11

Wal-Mart Founder
Sam Walton

He Learned From Competitors And
Then Went His Own Way

Sam Walton felt sick to his stomach. It was 1950, and he'd just spent five years turning his first store — a five-and-dime Ben Franklin franchise in Newport, Ark. — from a dying money-loser into the most profitable Ben Franklin in the six-state region.

Now he had to sell it.

His landlord refused to renew his five-year lease, because he wanted to give the now-thriving business to his son. Walton had nowhere else to move the store in Newport. So he sold it.

"It really was like a nightmare," Walton wrote in his 1992 autobiography, *Sam Walton: Made in America.* "I had built the best variety store in the whole region and worked hard in the community — done everything right — and now I was being kicked out of town."

Walton (1918–92) called it the low point of his business life. But he didn't dwell on his misfortune. Instead, he moved his wife, Helen, and their four small children to Bentonville, Ark., and bought a new store (this time with a 99-year lease).

"I had to pick myself up and get on with it, do it all over again, only even better this time," he wrote.

Do it better he did. That new store was the start of what became the biggest retailer in the world — Wal-Mart Stores Inc.

Walton's will to turn setbacks into opportunities was just one of the secrets behind the building of his venture, which reached

the $100 billion annual-sales mark in 1997. In five years, that num-
ber more than doubled to $218 billion. Wal-Mart made Walton
rich, and it changed the face of retailing. As of 2003, the company
operates more than 4,000 stores worldwide. In 1999, with
1,140,000 associates, Wal-Mart became the largest private
employer in the world.

Here are some of Walton's other secrets:

- **Keep trying to improve.** "If you ask Sam, 'How's business?'
  he's never satisfied," said Bernie Marcus, co-founder of
  Home Depot, in *Made in America*.

  For example, in 1966, Walton had five Wal-Mart
  stores in tiny towns, and they were doing a booming
  $10 million in annual sales. But he kept looking for
  ways to improve and expand his business and make it
  more efficient.

  He began reading about computers and became so
  excited about the possibilities that he enrolled in an IBM
  Corp. school and hired some computer experts.

  That early emphasis on technology turned out to be
  one of the keys to Wal-Mart's huge expansion.

  His constant quest for improvement and growth also
  led him to create Wal-Mart Supercenters, which have
  both groceries and general merchandise, and Sam's Club
  warehouse stores.

- **Happy employees mean happy customers.** "In the beginning, I was so chintzy I really didn't pay my employees
  well," Walton said.

  But soon he realized he had to give more to workers,
  whom he called "associates."

  "The way management treats associates is exactly
  how the associates will treat the customers," he said. "If
  the associates treat the customers well, the customers will
  return again and again, and that is where the real profit
  in this business lies."

  Although Walton continued to pay lower wages than
  the industry average, he started a profit-sharing program
  and let workers buy stock at a discount.

He also shared information and responsibility. Even clerks knew their store's purchases, profits, sales and markdowns.

He listened to the associates, too. He often visited stores and asked them for their suggestions.

"The folks on the front lines — the ones who actually talk to the customer — are the ones who really know what's going on out there," he said. "You'd better find out what they know."

- **Learn from the competition.** Walton was relentless about scrutinizing competitors. He'd walk into Kmart with a yellow legal pad or tape recorder, quizzing clerks about what and how much they ordered.

  But he didn't study rivals just so he could underprice them. He learned from them.

  Even at his first Ben Franklin store in Newport, Walton constantly visited the competing store across the street. He looked at prices, displays and the way it did business.

  And when he began discounting, he visited every discount store and company headquarters he knew of to learn more about how it worked.

  "We're really not concerned with what [competitors] are doing wrong; we're concerned with what they're doing right," he told managers. "Everyone is doing something right."

- **Do things your own way.** Although you should learn from competitors, don't follow them blindly, Walton advised.

  "Ignore the conventional wisdom," he said. "If everybody else is doing it one way, there's a good chance you can find your niche by going in exactly the opposite direction.

  "But be prepared for a lot of folks to wave you down and tell you you're headed the wrong way."

  For example, Walton ignored the conventional wisdom of his time — that towns with populations under 50,000 couldn't support a discount store for too long. Big retailers like Target and Kmart ignored these towns.

That let Wal-Mart grow for years without competition from any giant national discounters.

- **Be your own worst critic.** Walton knew that Wal-Mart had serious problems with merchandising and buying in its early days. One of the reasons the company survived, he said, is that he and the store managers constantly critiqued themselves.

  "When somebody made a bad mistake — whether it was myself or anybody else — we talked about it, admitted it, tried to figure out how to correct it, and then moved on to the next day's work," he wrote.

- **Lighten up.** Walton took his business seriously, but he wasn't afraid to laugh at himself. A little fun once in a while also kept customers, associates and shareholders happy.

  For example, to keep managers from revolting against his required Saturday morning meetings, he'd try to make them fun. Sometimes he'd have surprise visitors, such as (General Electric Chief Executive) Jack Welch or singer Garth Brooks. Another time he had an executive sing "Red River Valley."

  The tactic worked — he kept managers' interest, and business still got done.

  When Wal-Mart first came public, few shareholders — institutional or individual — would attend the annual shareholder meetings. But when the company turned the meetings into events, featuring golf and tennis and river float outings, attendance soared.

  "Loosen up, and everybody around you will loosen up," Walton said. "Have fun. Show enthusiasm — always."

- **Do what you love.** Showing enthusiasm is easy if you love your work. And Walton loved retailing.

  "I really love to pick an item — maybe the most basic merchandise — and then call attention to it," he wrote. "We would buy huge quantities of something

and dramatize it. We used to say you could sell anything if you hung it from the ceiling."

Because Walton loved his work, long hours weren't
drudgery. He often started his day at the office at 4:30
a.m. When his family traveled on vacations, he insisted
on stopping at all the local discount stores, so he could
see what they were up to.

"If you love your work, you'll be out there every day
trying to do it the best you possibly can, and pretty soon
everybody around will catch the passion from you —
like a fever," he said.

That passion also gives you energy to recover from
setbacks. Remember Walton's first store in Newport,
Ark., which he was forced to sell?

In 1969, he opened a Wal-Mart in Newport and competed with
the Ben Franklin store, run by his former landlord's son. The Wal-
Mart thrived. The Ben Franklin went out of business.

12

Paychex's Thomas Golisano

Built Business By Hiring For Guts
Instead Of Know-How

Thomas Golisano doesn't much care what training you have. It's drive he's after.

"We'll take attitude over skill level anytime," said Golisano, the chief executive of Paychex Inc., a provider of payroll and related services. "We believe people that have the right attitudes, and are motivated, will adapt to the skill level required. But if you have employees that are not motivated, that are not intense, you'll never teach them the skills."

He might well be right. Golisano's philosophy helped Paychex maintain its earnings even in the bearish economy of the early 2000s. In 2002, revenues were up 15%, and net income was up 9%, a showing that helped put Paychex among the top 20 favorite stocks of the National Association of Investors Corporation.

In a 2002 *Forbes* ranking, Golisano came in No. 1 among chief executives who do the best for their shareholders while receiving a reasonable compensation, taking into consideration the company's overall performance. Since coming public in 1983, Paychex provided its shareholders with a tidy 33% average annual return. Golisano's 2001 total compensation was about $936,000, according to *BusinessWeek's* executive compensation scoreboard, less than 0.4% of the company's nearly $255 million in net income.

Golisano's hiring philosophy grew out of his early experiences looking for entrepreneurs for Paychex partnerships and franchises, which have since been reabsorbed. After starting Paychex in 1971 with one employee and $3,000, he made deals with folks from all walks of life. Teachers, sales reps, engineers . . . they all had one thing in common: motivation. By 2003 Rochester, N.Y.–based Paychex served more than 440,000 clients from more than 100 locations.

"He and a lot of us have come to understand that you can teach ability — you can't teach attitude," concurred Gene Polisseni, Paychex's marketing vice president. "Attitude is something they walk through the front door with."

In addition to drive and energy, Golisano looks for a track record that highlights resourcefulness and a willingness to take risks. That entrepreneurial spirit has helped Paychex expand far beyond cutting checks. As legislators continue to create regulatory headaches for small employers, Golisano has mined a vast, untapped market.

"[More than] 30% of our clients have four employees or less," Golisano said. "They're not buying our service because we can write four payroll checks. They're buying our service because we keep them in compliance with the federal and state governments."

He's also boosted his product line by learning and culling from other industries. For example, he bases his product and service rollouts on the same techniques used by companies that make consumer staples, such as tissues.

"Instead of doing a lot of market research, he'll have a tendency to try something out on a limited basis," said G. Thomas Clark, a longtime Paychex executive and former board member who is now retired. "When you have a wide branch network, it's very easy to try something out in one area."

That's how Paychex introduced a MasterCard that allows employees to get cash and charge purchases against their pay.

He started an automatic tax-filing and payment service after watching a competitor try it first.

"You don't always have to be the pioneer," Golisano said. "You just have to eventually do it better than everybody else."

Said Polisseni, "Tom's outlook is, there's a pothole in every road, but every pothole is repairable — and let's not sit here and think of all the reasons something won't work; let's think about why something will work."

Golisano's penchant for experimenting and tinkering with new products is helped along by the high profitability of the base payroll business, according to Smith Barney analyst Keith Mullins.

"It gives him the cash flow to test and monitor a lot of different things," Mullins said.

But the flow of new products, and of new state and federal regulations that firms have to follow, creates a challenge for Golisano. The man who hires for attitude has to keep employees up to speed on complex issues.

According to *Training* magazine's 2002 Training Top 100, each Paychex employee receives an average of 146 hours of training per year, more than twice the 63-hour average per organization rated. Paychex came in No. 58 in that annual survey of companies across the nation, ranked according to their investment in workforce development.

"We go to the *n*th degree on that," said Golisano, who has an associate degree in business from the State University of New York at Alfred.

Golisano, who also ran for New York governor on the Independent ticket (1994, 1998, 2002), was moved to start Paychex when he was a sales manager at a payroll processing company that served big companies. He couldn't convince his bosses that small business was a worthwhile market for payroll work, so at age 29 he struck out on his own to serve small firms in New York state. His success seemed far from assured in the beginning.

"The first four years in Rochester, I was barely surviving," Golisano said. Within less than three decades, he was the city's only billionaire.

After the company took root, other people approached him, asking to start branches in other cities as joint-venture partners or franchisees.

He agreed, and the firm spread to 19 other cities. In 1979, Golisano persuaded his partners and franchise-holders to merge their locations back into the parent company, which went public in 1983.

13

McDonald's Ray Kroc
He Cooked Up A Winner

Ray Kroc believed that never was a good time to stop growing. Kroc (1902–84) was already 52 years old when he got the franchising rights to a small hamburger stand started by Dick and Mac McDonald in San Bernardino, Calif. He'd been running a successful business, selling milkshake mixers.

"Yet I was alert to other opportunities," Kroc wrote (with Robert Anderson) in *Grinding It Out: The Making of McDonald's.*

"I have a saying that goes, 'As long as you're green you're growing. As soon as you're ripe you start to rot.'"

Kroc pursued growth with a vengeance. He turned that franchise agreement into the largest fast food chain in the world.

Growing up, Kroc wasn't an avid student. Instead, he spent his time daydreaming about his future and his future success. "I'd imagine all kinds of situations and how I would handle them," Kroc wrote. But they weren't idle fantasies he conjured.

"I never considered my dreams wasted energy; they were invariably linked to some form of action," Kroc wrote. "When I dreamed about having a lemonade stand, for example, it wasn't long before I set up a lemonade stand."

Smiles Are Good Business

That lemonade stand was the first in a long series of jobs. Kroc took a lesson from almost every one. For example, working behind the lunch counter at his uncle's drugstore soda fountain, he discovered the importance of a positive attitude in sales. "That's where I learned you could influence people with a smile and enthusiasm and sell them a sundae when what they'd come for was a cup of coffee," he said.

It was at a job selling ribbon novelties that Kroc discovered the art of tailoring his spiel to the needs of his customers. "I'd have a sample room set up in whatever hotel I was staying in, and I'd learn what each buyer's taste was and sell to it," he said. "No self-respecting pitcher throws the same way to every batter, and no self-respecting salesman makes the same pitch to every client."

While selling paper goods for the Lilly Cup Co., he saw that customers appreciated a straightforward, brief approach. "They would buy if I made my pitch and asked for their order without a lot of beating around the bush," he said. "The key to closing a sale is to know when to stop selling.

"Too many salesmen, I found, would make a good presentation and convince the client, but they couldn't recognize that critical moment when they should have stopped talking."

In 1938 he signed a deal to be the exclusive sales agent for the MultiMixer, a milkshake mixer that could handle five shakes at once. It meant giving up a steady income, but Kroc believed he could make it work. He told a group of graduate students at Dartmouth College you can achieve anything if you set your mind to it.

"You're not going to get it free, and you have to take risks. I don't mean daredevil risks. But you have to take risks, and in some case you must go for broke," he said. "If you believe in something, you've got to be in it to the end of your toes. Taking reasonable risk is part of the challenge."

Adversity Built Strength

It wasn't easy. He had to take an unwanted partner to get the business started, and buying out the partner later put a severe strain on the company's resources. Rather than get irritated about it, Kroc chose to look on the upside. "Perhaps without that adversity I might not have been able to persevere later on when my financial burdens were redoubled," he said. "I learned then how to keep problems from crushing me."

Kroc opened his first McDonald's in Des Plaines, Ill., in 1955. After he ironed out early problems, the concept caught on. As he increased the number of franchises, Kroc had to add staff. He had specific qualifications in mind when he looked for them.

He never looked for yes men. He wanted people willing to disagree. "I believe that if two executives think the same, one of them is superfluous," he said.

Once hired, a Kroc employee was delegated authority to do his or her job. One early executive, Harry Sonneborn, came up with an unusual lease-to-purchase deal to acquire future store sites. Kroc thought the idea was crazy.

"But I let Harry plunge ahead without interference," Kroc said. "I believe if you hire a man to do a job, you ought to get out of the way and let him do it. If you doubt his ability, you shouldn't have hired him in the first place."

Similarly, when Sonneborn hired an expensive consultant, others in the office were certain Kroc would be angry. "But that was the farthest thing from my mind," he wrote. "I know that you have to spend money to make money, and as far as I was concerned, Harry was simply doing the job I'd hired him to do."

In 1967, all the economists were predicting a recession; most businesses planned cutbacks in construction. Not Kroc. He ordered expansion to proceed.

"Hell's bells, when times are bad is when you want to build," Kroc said. "Why wait for things to pick up so everything will cost you more? If a location is good enough to buy, we want to build on it right away and be in there before the competition."

As the company became more successful, it required larger stores with seating. Some on the executive team urged caution. Kroc, however, was thinking big. "I believe that if you think small, you'll stay small," Kroc said.

Over the course of his career, Kroc had to spend major cash to steer his company where he wanted it to go. He bought out the McDonald brothers' share of the business.

"I don't stew about what the other guy is making in a deal like this," he said. "I'm concerned about whether it's going to be a good thing for McDonald's."

14

Tupperware's Brownie Wise
Built And Prepped Her Army With
Methodical Goal Setting

Too many people strive to achieve their goals too soon, Brownie Wise said. All she asked for was a small victory every day.

Those wins became a big triumph for Earl Tupper, inventor of Tupperware.

When Tupper introduced his plastic food containers to the public in 1945, they fell flat and stayed that way for six years.

He faced three major problems: The public didn't trust plastic; it didn't know how to use Tupperware products; and he was a recluse who didn't know how to manage a sales force.

The solution to his problems presented itself in 1951 in the person of Brownie Wise. That year she was selling two truckloads of products a week as an independent dealer who used home parties to market the items. Tupper couldn't help but notice her and invited her to company headquarters to discover her secret.

As Wise explained to Tupper, the only way to sell his products was by demonstrating them. The airtight containers, for example, had a patented seal that was tricky to use. He recruited her on the spot to perfect and roll out the Tupperware Party direct-selling method.

Long before Wise (1913–92) won national recognition as the force behind the company's success, she was a struggling divorcee, raising a sickly son on her own. She tried out party sales to bring in extra money.

Her first attempt was a disaster. When Wise made her first in-home sales presentation, she became nauseated by nervousness, tripped over her display case and left the hostess' house with a bloody nose.

On another occasion, she made her pitch in a living room filled with cages of singing canaries and had to shout to be heard. During yet another tough session, a bulldog wandered in wearing glasses. Wise, who was under a lot of stress at the time (her son was in the hospital), was certain she was hallucinating, but persevered. Only later did she learn the dog was nearsighted.

The only way to gain poise, she learned, was through experience.

Tupper gave Wise carte blanche to build a sales force to her liking. In shaping it, Wise never forgot her own experiences.

She ruled no one out when assessing potential dealers. For example, when a poorly dressed woman showed up in a coal delivery truck that had belonged to her deceased husband, Wise ignored her appearance and looked at the desire in her eyes.

She tried constantly to stay on the lookout.

"I stopped at the same gasoline station several times," she recalled in a 1954 interview with *BusinessWeek*, "with my station wagon loaded with Tupperware. The station man got curious, asked me about it. It wound up with his wife putting on a party."

In recruiting large numbers of new dealers, Wise's major problem was that most were untrained in and apprehensive about sales.

Her motto: "Build people, and they will build the business for you."

She included in her formal training a Dale Carnegie course in public speaking and tips on how to make presentations, such as how to offer premiums to prospective hostesses. She insisted the presenter have a look of determination on her face and hold her head erect.

But it was her personal seminars, characterized as training session, circus and revival meeting all rolled into one, that truly inspired her people.

Wise's speeches had such a strong moral theme that clergymen would come to meetings to hear her. Consider her advice on setting goals, which she outlined in her 1957 book, *Best Wishes:* "First, ask yourself if your desire for this thing is great enough that you would work hard to get it. Second, will this thing honestly be good for you and the people around you?

"And last, is there anyone who could possibly be hurt by this wish coming true?"

She attributed her approach to her grandmother, who raised seven children on her own.

Wise also taught her salespeople to focus on a single goal. "The human being is so constructed that he can focus best on only one thing."

While at Tupperware, Wise was often asked what her hobbies were; she didn't have any until she retired in 1958.

To never lose sight of your goal, she recommended visualizing it.

One of her early goals was to own her own home. "I found a picture that most resembled the house we wanted to build, and I hung this picture on the wall, where I could look up at any time and see this home," she said.

The insightful Wise realized that most people are impatient and want to attain their goals immediately. Instead, she advised seeking a small victory daily and monitoring progress.

"Plan on progress," Wise wrote. "Perhaps you will set a certain time each week, and maybe in some cases, each day, to go off by yourself and write down the progress you've made. Whether you write it down or make a mental note of the ground you've covered, it is important that you keep a chart of progress.

"Mechanical reminders are often very helpful to keep from getting enmeshed in the details of the day and losing sight of the specific things you must do toward your goal."

Wise applied the same concepts — visualizing a goal and taking a step-by-step approach to attaining it — to motivating her sales representatives; she gave them a specific career path with set milestones and flashy awards.

A dealer who recruited four other dealers became a unit manager and was entitled to larger commissions. The next level was branch manager, and then came the ultimate goal: recruiting enough dealers to become a full-fledged distributor. This grass-roots recruitment process met with huge success. In 1951 there were only 200 dealers. In 1954 that number had exploded to 9,000.

As for more immediate rewards, top dealers received Cadillacs and other gifts at splashy promotional events — gifts the other reps wouldn't soon forget.

Whenever obstacles presented themselves, Wise always invoked the memory of someone who'd overcome greater adversity. For her, it was Helen Keller. "When I think of the life of Helen Keller," she wrote, "I feel ashamed to even write the word 'impossible.'"

Another exercise she recommended to overcome setbacks and regain confidence was to talk about your positive attributes. "Brag about the many talents you possess and what big things you can accomplish, simply by putting a few of them to work," she said.

If someone were apprehensive about a coming event or what the future might hold, she believed that just talking about the fear would dispel it.

In a trick to catch her people's imagination and further instill confidence, Wise, who at her peak traveled more than 175,000 miles annually, carried a magic charm with her. That charm was a raw block of polyethylene from which Tupperware is made. She encouraged her salespeople to rub it for good luck.

15

Radio Shack's Charles Tandy

His Commonsense Approach Built An Electronics Giant

Charles Tandy was willing to fight for what he believed in.

Tandy, chairman of Tandy Corp., which operated leather craft stores, wanted to buy Radio Shack, a Boston-based chain of nine electronics stores, in 1963.

Radio Shack was on the edge of bankruptcy, but Tandy had studied the company for some months. His research convinced him the problem was poor management and that Radio Shack was a turnaround opportunity.

His fellow board members, however, were not nearly as certain. They were reluctant to go along. According to Irvin Farman, author of *Tandy's Money Machine*, Tandy was sure his instincts were right.

When coaxing and facts fail, sometimes hardball is the only method that works, Tandy felt.

"If I don't get an affirmative vote on this," Tandy told the board, "then I will sell every share of stock I own in the corporation, and I will, personally, take this on my own hook."

Knowing that would've destroyed Fort Worth, Texas–based Tandy Corp.'s financial footing, the board acceded to Tandy's wishes and bought Radio Shack.

Tandy (1918–78) proved he was right. In 2000, the year the company was renamed RadioShack Corp., it had more than 7,100 company-owned and franchised stores and sales of nearly $4.8 billion.

Buying Radio Shack wasn't the first time that Tandy saw opportunity where others didn't. In fact, he found opportunity everywhere — even in military hospitals.

Tandy's father was a partner in Hinckley-Tandy Leather Co. of Fort Worth, a small company in the shoe findings business. That was the business of wholesalers who provided leather heels, shoelaces and polish to shoe repair shops in the region. It was a steady if unspectacular business.

However, while serving in the South Pacific as a naval officer during World War II, young Tandy noticed that wounded soldiers and sailors were given crafts to keep them busy and to serve as therapy.

He saw an opportunity and wrote his father from Hawaii suggesting that the business branch out into leather crafts. That advice — which his father took — ultimately led to the formation of what became Tandy Corp.

When he found one opportunity, Tandy tried to turn it into more. After he returned from the military in 1948, Tandy decided the new leather craft business offered the perfect chance to test some of the other business ideas he had percolating in his head. He asked for and received permission to run the business. He opened two retail stores in 1950 to supplement the mail-order trade begun by his father.

Charles soon began to absorb on-the-job lessons, including this one: Learn from your mistakes.

His father, David, gave Charles money to buy dyes for leathers. Without thinking carefully, he bought 10 bottles of every dye available. Soon, he ran out of the most popular colors, such as white, and was left with a large supply of other colors, such as purple.

"To this day, when I'm thinking about inventory, I always ask myself if I have enough white dye or too much purple," Tandy said later.

He believed ownership was a great motivator. When a manager opened a Tandy Leather store, he was required to put up 25% of the $10,000 it took to get started in return for 25% of the store's profits. If a prospective manager didn't have the money, Tandy would guarantee the loan.

"If a guy has his own money tied up in a store, he's going to work a lot of extra hours, not for you, not for the company, but for himself," Tandy said. "Why? Because it's his own money that's at risk. And he knows that if he loses it, it's gone for good."

Tandy had a simple formula for locating his stores: Put them where the customers are. He tracked where his mail orders came from. Once he decided on a city, he tried to place his store on one of the best-known streets in town. It didn't have to be the main street or even a retail street, but it did have to be one that was known. For example, he opened stores on Mission Street in San Francisco and Pacific Street in Dallas.

Yet he was careful about financing. His instructions to managers when they set up new stores was straightforward: "Find a street in town that everybody knows, and then keep walking on that street until you come to where we can afford the rent."

Tandy was optimistic, telling himself that he could accomplish anything. He tried to pass his enthusiasm along to others.

"He had the ability really to inspire you, to make you dream, to make you believe that he was going to [accomplish] everything he said he would," said Lloyd Redd, manager of a Tandy Leather store in Omaha, Neb., as cited in *Tandy's Money Machine.*

Tandy wanted honest opinions. To get them, he used to revel in playing devil's advocate. He'd say outrageous things in order to draw a reaction, board member Phil North told biographer Farman. "He wanted you to defend your position or contrary view."

By the same token, Tandy recognized he didn't know everything. He trusted people he hired to be more familiar with their areas of special knowledge than he was. "He let them run that part of their jobs," North said. "He didn't try to run everything."

Tandy believed one could learn a lot by asking questions. When he bought Radio Shack, he asked people from executives to suppliers about aspects of his new business.

"I don't know nothin' about electronics," he said at the time. "I just know about business. I'm just a businessman. It pays to be dumb, to ask questions."

By asking questions, for example, he was able to get enough information to wrangle a good deal from a radio tube manufacturer.

In the process, he learned that comparison-shopping often brings better prices. He got in touch with all the major manufacturers of radio tubes about securing better prices, and they all came back with the same numbers.

"All except Raytheon, because Raytheon wasn't on our shelf, you see," Tandy said. "And that's one of the first things you need to do.

Find a guy who is not getting any of your business, and he's more anxious to talk to you."

Tandy knew the importance of having good relationships with suppliers. To keep them that way, he insisted that bills be paid when they arrived.

In fact, according to John McDaniel, a former accounting executive for the company, Tandy was so anxious to build good relations with suppliers that even when money was tight he refused to hold off making payments.

"In the early days, he didn't even want us to hold [a bill] until two days before it was due, because he thought we might be one day late if we did that," McDaniel said.

Perhaps more than anything else, Tandy believed that a man's reach should exceed his grasp. As he achieved one goal, he set new ones higher than what he'd just achieved. When he first rejoined his father's company after leaving the military, his aim was "to build a company with sales of $1 million."

Once he achieved that, he decided: "If I could earn $1 million before taxes, I'd be doing good. My next goal was $100 million volume. Now it's a billion. I have learned to move the figures far enough away."

16

Retailer
Charles R. Walgreen Sr.
His Innovations Helped Build Nation's
Biggest Drugstore Chain

Charles R. Walgreen Sr. wanted his small Chicago pharmacy to give patrons fast service that would wow them.

Every pharmacy at the turn of the century supplied prescriptions. Every pharmacy delivered. But what if his delivered faster?

He decided to use new technology — the telephone — to boost his business. When a nearby customer telephoned an order for some nonprescription goods, Walgreen (1873–1939) slowly repeated both the order and the caller's address out loud.

Then Caleb Danner, the store's handyman, would listen, collect and wrap the items quickly.

As Danner darted to the caller's home, Walgreen stretched the conversation for several more minutes, talking about anything under the sun.

This gave Danner time to land at the caller's doorstep, interrupt the phone call and hand the unsuspecting customer the items ordered minutes before on the phone. Soon, she'd spread the word about the extraordinary service.

The "two-minute stunt" and other innovations helped Walgreen change the face of pharmacies and build what became America's largest drugstore chain. A hundred years after Walgreen opened his first store, the company that still bears his name had sales of $24.6 billion in 3,520 stores.

Opened First Store In 1901

When Walgreen opened his first shop, on the corner of Cottage Grove and Bowen avenues on Chicago's South Side in 1901, drugstores were drab and dimly lit. Customers stopped to find what they needed and left.

Hidden in the back of the store was the pharmacist, working behind a wooden grillwork partition and surrounded by bottles of compounds, a mortar and pestle and a jar of leeches.

Walgreen saw an opportunity. Most drugstores had small soda fountains. At first, they sold bottled soda water as a health aid. Later, they added flavors, such as lemon, strawberry and pineapple, and began featuring a small soda fountain apparatus inside their front counter.

Walgreen saw a way to innovate: Why not make the fountains large enough to seat customers at tables and serve treats including ice-cream sodas, phosphates and sundaes?

Walgreen took action after a shop adjacent to his second drugstore became vacant. He rented the space and cut an archway through the common wall. He installed a 16-foot-long marble-top fountain and a 12-foot mirror bordered by intricate woodwork against the far wall.

He also added eight small tables and as many booths, wrote Herman and Rick Kogan in *Pharmacist to the Nation: A History of Walgreen Co.*

But Walgreen knew that ice-cream parlors weren't entirely new in the Midwest metropolis. He looked for an edge.

He knew customers appreciated high quality. So he developed a private-label ice-cream brand for the store that had a higher percentage of butterfat than the ice cream from his suppliers. His ice cream was always fresh, because it could be made in minutes in the store's basement.

The soda fountain was a huge success. Customer traffic slumped, however, after summer ended.

Walgreen analyzed the situation — he had space to serve ice cream, but people didn't want it when the weather was cold.

So he created a new market. Walgreen persuaded his wife, Myrtle, to cook. She fed customers through the winter with a different hot soup, sandwich and dessert menu every day from Monday to Saturday. It worked, and the fountain stayed busy year-round.

The Rio, Ill., native encouraged his employees to innovate, too. In fact, one of the store's fountain managers in 1922 came up with the fountain's greatest hit — the milkshake.

He'd seen how much people liked ice cream, so he created a double-rich chocolate malted milk thickened with three scoops of vanilla ice cream and topped by whipped cream and a cherry. It came with a complimentary package of vanilla cookies.

It didn't take long before customers began standing three and four deep at the counter to get their taste of what's now an American classic.

Walgreen expanded product offerings and came up with new ways to boost sales to customers attracted to the store. The Perfume Bar allowed female customers to sample many famous brands while men inspected the cases of cigars and pipe tobaccos. "Concentrations," or striking displays of a specific product, were placed in highly visible areas of the store.

Walgreen also poured energy and time into developing other private-label products — from "Sure Death Bug Pizen" for killing bedbugs to freshly roasted coffee beans to cold cream.

To make sure customers were confident in the house products, the store guaranteed in writing that no item would carry the Walgreen name if it didn't meet high quality standards.

Walgreen also knew customers flocked to sales but felt that too many sales made a store look cheap. Why not offer everyday discounts on some items? The strategy could work if he bought in bulk. So he persuaded other neighborhood pharmacy owners to pool their purchases of the same products. Walgreen became president of the Velvet Club and successfully negotiated with suppliers for lower wholesale prices.

Back then, the concept was so radical that people questioned whether the $1 Gillette razors that sold for 69 cents at Walgreen's were indeed genuine.

"Don't be afraid of anything sold at a Walgreen store, for quantity buying permits low prices, and we often sell the equal of gold dollars for less than 100 cents," Walgreen said in the chain's newsletter, *The Pepper Pod*.

Realizing that customers shopped where they felt most comfortable, Walgreen launched *The Pepper Pod* in December 1919 to interact more closely with patrons. He made sure the 12-page newsletter included something for everyone. Articles included "Beauty Hints," "Christmas Suggestions" and "Constipation and How to Prevent It."

Customers were thrilled. Walgreen encouraged them to contribute to the publication, thus deepening their loyalty. One article by a customer carried the headline "Germany of Today" in heavy block letters and gave a firsthand account of post-World War I Berlin.

Walgreen didn't stick to the tried and true. Although other drugstores didn't advertise heavily, he began distributing circulars in 1921 showing photos and addresses of all 25 stores. On Nov. 16, 1922, the company's first full-page newspaper ad appeared in the *Chicago Tribune* to inform readers of "Chicago's Leading Drug Sale Thursday, Friday, Saturday."

He also knew how to take an advantage of an opportunity. He saw how popular radio was becoming. Walgreens became the first drugstore chain to advertise on the air.

Ads Touted Prices

Walgreen made sure ads focused strictly on dates of special sales campaigns; locations of nearby stores; illustrations and descriptions of products; and prices, which were in larger type than the name of the product itself. No space or airtime was used to make pledges of excellent service.

Why not? He wanted his customers to come into a Walgreen store and actually experience the service. To ensure that it would be top-notch, Walgreen wrote employee manuals on cleanliness, the importance of smiling and good sales skills.

He even listed ways to handle a preoccupied or worried customer: "Express a real sympathy and understanding in your dealings. . . . Don't try to distract his attention from his worries by talking unnecessarily."

Walgreen wanted employees to always make that extra effort. In a book called *Set Your Sales for Bigger Earnings*, Walgreen provided more tips on how to give the best service.

One illustration showed a smiling, clean-cut salesclerk tying up a stack of items in a neat bundle. The explanation said, "Little extra services are the cheapest kind of advertising that merely takes thought and a few seconds of time!"

"Success," Walgreen wrote in the same book, "is doing a thousand little things the right way — doing many of them over and over again."

17

Barney Creator Sheryl Leach

She Relied On Common Sense To Help Her Build A Purple Empire

Sheryl Leach was frustrated. Her 2-year-old son, Patrick, was driving her nuts with his unlimited energy. He had no interest in anything for more than five minutes — except a children's video, *We Sing Together.*

Patrick loved to watch the video over and over. It was fun and educational. But now he'd seen the video so many times he needed something more advanced.

Leach tried to buy a follow-up video, but there wasn't one. A sequel was planned, and there was a long waiting list to buy it. Nothing else on the market was appropriate for very small children.

Stuck in traffic one day in 1987, Leach analyzed the problem. She knew there had to be millions of parents out there in the same situation. Why not make a video herself?

"When I had the idea, it was almost as if I could see into the future, and I saw pieces of a puzzle zoomed into place and already completed," Leach said in a 1999 interview. The completed "puzzle" Leach envisioned would be entertaining and educational while imparting a strong moral message.

Barney The Teddy Bear?

Leach, a former teacher and free-lance writer living in the Dallas area, figured out a plot. At first, she made the lead a teddy bear that came to life to play with children. Then she took her son to a dinosaur exhibit and saw how fascinated he was. She also remembered how her former students loved dinosaurs.

She shifted her focus to attract the market she was sure was out there. Barney the dinosaur was born.

That shift proved to be inspired. When Lyrick Corp., owner of *Barney the Dinosaur*, was bought by children's programming producer HIT Entertainment for $275 million in 2001, it had sold over 65 million Barney home videos. London-based HIT also owns the popular *Bob the Builder* series.

The *Barney & Friends* television show has been one of the top-rated programs for children under 6 since its debut in 1992, and stage shows have sold out in dozens of cities. More than 100 million Barney books, several of which were bestsellers, had been sold at the time of the parent company's acquisition.

Barney products — including toys, games, apparel, accessories and even snack foods — are selling worldwide.

After she came up with the idea, Leach realized she didn't have experience producing children's videos. So she relied on common sense.

"There's a logic, a rhyme and reason the way business operates and the way human beings operate," she said.

She knew she had a place to do the job — her father-in-law had just built a video studio. She looked for an experienced video production team. She found local actors to play the parts she wrote out. She designed Barney's purple costume — kids love purple — and hired a seamstress to put it together.

Leach also did her research. She and her team identified 17 key elements to make Barney appealing.

Although a number of them remain secret, "Some things are very self-evident," Leach said. "All parents know very young children love to watch other children; everyone knows children love music; and I think having our characters say and do things that are familiar to the child are all essential."

Leach's enthusiasm persuaded her father-in-law to back the project, and the first Barney video was produced in 1988.

All that was left was to market the videos. But how? After the video was produced, not enough money remained to hire an ad agency. Leach turned to a group she could trust — neighborhood moms who volunteered to help.

"We were all moms and in the trenches together," Leach said. "It was just natural to ask [them]."

The campaigners called themselves "Mom Blitzers" and used a two-pronged strategy. First, they called stores culled from a list Leach purchased and offered them the chance to sell the videos. As a sweetener, if the videos the stores purchased didn't sell, they could send them back.

The campaigners created demand through the second prong, called "Operation Preschool." They sent copies of the video to preschools and day-care centers near video and toy stores carrying the Barney videos.

Leach's marketing strategy worked perfectly, and Barney became a star in the Dallas area. Then his fame spread across the country.

To make sure he stayed a star, Leach kept a careful eye on quality. "We only license products that are near and dear to our target audience," Leach said.

"Even during our very expansive growth, we held our licensees to about 35, whereas other properties have hundreds," she said. "And today we still have just about the same amount as we did then," she said in 1999.

While Barney is hugely popular with children, many adults and parents label the character "mind-numbing."

But Leach ignored the critics and kept coming up with new videos. "There are always people who want to knock it down or make fun," she said. "But our overriding concern is that we have children's welfare at heart and that we're true to the reason we came up with Barney in the first place."

A desire to help others is a key to any success, says Leach, who was supervising a new Barney TV series for HIT in 2001.

"It seems to me that there's a natural force that goes into play to help you when you're doing something for a higher purpose," she said. "If you're doing something that serves yourself only, you won't get the same help, satisfaction or rewards. If you can find something to do that serves mankind, you'll have [the] wind at your back."

18

Bank Of America's
A. P. Giannini

His Focus On Ordinary People
Helped Build A Financial Goliath

Amadeo Peter Giannini knew what it was to be a working man, to get up early every morning and come home late at night, bone-weary. The problem: None of his fellow board members at Columbus Savings & Loan in San Francisco did.

Giannini (1870–1949) joined the board in 1902 but soon found himself at loggerheads with the other directors. As a one-time laborer, Giannini wanted the savings and loan to market services for ordinary people who were struggling to make something of their lives. He saw an untapped market.

The other directors, however, were more concerned with the carriage trade, the traditional and almost exclusive market for banks. After two years of struggling to have his views heard, Giannini decided he couldn't take it anymore and resigned.

"I'll start my own bank," he declared.

He set up shop almost immediately. His determination led to the Bank of Italy, later the Bank of America, which at one time was the largest bank in the world.

"It's no use . . . to decide what's going to happen unless you have the courage of your convictions," he said. "Many a brilliant idea has been lost because the man who dreamed it lacked the spunk or the spine to put it across.

"It doesn't matter if you don't always hit the exact bull's-eye," he said. "The other rings in the targets score points, too."

Giannini was born in San Jose, Calif., the son of immigrants from Genoa, Italy. When Amadeo was 7, his father died. His mother remarried, and the family moved to San Francisco.

Amadeo was 12 years old when he went to work in his stepfather's produce business. He had to rise in the wee hours of the morning, well before school, and go to the San Francisco docks to await shipments. It was far from wasted time, though. He used the time he waited to think about his future and how he wanted to approach it.

Even at this young age, Giannini was already developing what was to become the prevailing philosophy of his business life.

"I decided that a man who wants to reach the top must keep his record clear," he said later. "He cannot do anything of which he is ashamed or that might bob up at some future time to embarrass him. I also concluded that you had to set up a mark to shoot at. Decide what you want — and then go after it, hammer and tongs."

Although a quick learner, Giannini quit school at 14 to work full time for his stepfather. He understood that to learn the ways of business, he needed to get firsthand experience he wasn't getting in the classroom.

Soon he was traveling up and down the California coast meeting with farmers. Although young, he knew to succeed he had to be straightforward with them or they wouldn't deal with him. He offered honest deals, good prices and respectful treatment, and he stood by his word.

His reputation — and the company's business — grew. His stepfather made him a full partner by the time he was 19. Just a dozen years later, the business had grown enough that Giannini sold his interest to employees with the intention of retiring.

However, the following year he joined the board of Columbus Savings & Loan. When he decided to start his own bank, Giannini borrowed $150,000 from his stepfather and 10 friends and opened the first branch of the Bank of Italy. It occupied a converted saloon across the street from Columbus Savings.

He didn't think of problems that sprang up as barriers. He looked at them as inspirations that spurred him on.

"I thrive on obstacles," he said in 1923, "particularly obstacles placed in my way by narrow-gauged competitors and their political friends."

From the beginning, Giannini showed a willingness to defy conventional wisdom. While banks at the time considered it unethical to solicit business, Giannini went door-to-door to convince prospective depositors of the soundness of his venture.

"I have always believed that if a business is worthwhile, it is worth seeking," he said.

After the 1906 San Francisco earthquake and fire, most banks remained shut to sort out the damage. Not the Bank of Italy. It set up shop on a plank placed on two barrels in the North Beach district and lent money to rebuild based on people's signatures and whether they had calluses on their hands — a sure sign, Giannini thought, that they were willing to work hard.

"We didn't lose a dollar," he said, "and we gained thousands of new friends."

Doing good was good business, he discovered.

"At the time of the fire, I was trying to make money for myself," he said. "But the fire cured me of that."

He made it his life's mission to use the power of banking to help others. In 1921 he opened a women's banking department. Though the prevailing wisdom in the industry was "Never loan money on anything that eats," he helped finance California's dairy, sheep and beef industries. Under his leadership, the institution became the state's largest agricultural lender.

Those innovations helped the Bank of Italy continue to grow. Giannini began opening branches, something that was unheard of at the time. In 1909, a Bank of Italy office opened in San Jose, and in 1913, he expanded to southern California. By 1920 he'd opened offices in New York City, making the Bank of Italy the first to do branch banking across state lines.

Giannini looked at how quickly his bank was growing and decided he needed to set up a holding company. In 1928, he formed TransAmerica Corp. as a holding company for his wide financial interests and, in the same year, purchased Bank of America, an old New York lending institution.

"The time to go ahead in business is when the other fellows aren't doing much," he said. He continued to expand.

As Julie Fenster points out in her book, *In the Words of Great Business Leaders*, Giannini's success didn't change his way of doing business.

"Even after Bank of America took its rank as the world's largest bank in 1940, Giannini's desk remained out in the open on the main floor," Fenster wrote. "He maintained standing orders that anyone — anyone — could come to see him, from a shareholder with a question to a fisherman looking for a loan."

Giannini believed he ran a tighter ship by being more open with customers and employees.

"I have found it quite possible to dispense with most of the trappings which many executives find necessary," he said. "Perhaps I do not impress people as much as I might. But of this I am convinced — I can accomplish more work without the trappings."

His approach to problem solving was similar — simple and direct. He'd concentrate on a problem and then shift his focus to other concerns for a while before re-examining the original problem. This, he said, gave him perspective.

"In working out any plan or idea, I use what you might call the intermittent method," he said. "I hit the problem hard, then leave it for a while, and later come back. This method permits me to bring to the particular problem many ideas that come from mature reflection."

19

Chewing Gum Mogul
William Wrigley Jr.
He Stuck To His Vision

When William Wrigley Jr. hit the road from Philadelphia to Chicago in 1891, he had just $32 in his pocket.

Yet he wasn't worried. He'd overcome worse obstacles. For instance, he'd been kicked out of school repeatedly. Low funds were just one more challenge.

And it was one he rose to. After founding the William Wrigley Jr. Co. that year, he spent the next few building his firm into a powerhouse that became the world's largest gum manufacturer. He later bought the Chicago Cubs, building championship teams, and developed Catalina Island in California as one of the nation's top resort destinations.

Wrigley (1861–1932) didn't have a smooth ride. As a child, he was adventurous. He ran away from home at age 11 and went to New York City. He wasn't unhappy at home; he simply wanted to prove that he could take care of himself. He got a job as a newsboy a few hours after he arrived, found a warm place on the street to sleep and stayed the summer.

He returned home and went to school but repeatedly got into scrapes. He was expelled an average of once every three weeks, according to a *Fortune* magazine article published in 1932. Finally, at age 13, he was permanently kicked out for throwing a pie at the school.

Wrigley figured he'd better learn to be good at something. So he threw all his efforts into becoming a salesman for his father's soap making company. Wrigley proved to be a natural.

He wouldn't take no for an answer. He sold one customer by asking for sales tips after the guy criticized Wrigley's technique. Another customer went to work at 6:45 a.m. each day; Wrigley got up early and bumped into him every day for a month as the man was opening his shop. The man finally bought soap from Wrigley.

Persistence

"Sticking is one of the big things in salesmanship," Wrigley said in the book *In the Words of Great Business Leaders* by Julie Fenster. "Nearly all buyers say 'No!' at first. Real salesmen stick until the buyer has used up his last 'No!'"

It wasn't just that attitude that carried Wrigley.

"For years there hung a sign over his desk: 'Nothing great was ever achieved without enthusiasm,'" wrote Peter Golenbock in *Wrigleyville.*

That enthusiasm made it easy for Wrigley to stay optimistic on his arrival in Chicago. He felt he could accomplish anything as long as he believed in himself.

"A man's doubts and fears are his worst enemies," Wrigley said in a company document. "He can go ahead and do anything so long as he doesn't know he can't do it."

He also was smart enough to outwit his rivals.

Wrigley's company in Chicago started out selling his father's soap. When competitors tried to undercut his prices, he gave free baking soda to his dealers for every box of soap they sold. That kind of incentive became a Wrigley hallmark. Soon enough, baking soda was in such demand, he began selling it.

Then he began offering chewing gum as an incentive. Demand for that grew so fast that Wrigley started selling gum under his own name in 1892. He launched Juicy Fruit and Wrigley's Spearmint in 1893.

There were a dozen chewing gum companies in the U.S. at the time, but Wrigley wouldn't be deterred. He kept his trademark optimism through good times and bad.

"I have never seen Mr. Wrigley worried," a Wrigley executive said in Fenster's book. "In crises that would have crushed many men, that had me running around in circles, he remained as calm, as cheerful as if he were on a Sunday picnic."

Wrigley personally visited customers, according to a Wrigley Co. profile. He believed that business, like life, was based on relationships.

Wrigley's great-grandson, Wrigley Co. Chief Executive Bill Wrigley Jr., talked in a speech about the elder Wrigley's belief in fairness.

A vendor came into Wrigley's office one day to sell him a promotional item.

After they negotiated a deal, the man said he'd lose money because Wrigley had made himself such a good deal. Wrigley tore up the contract and said, "We don't want to do business with anybody who loses money on us."

"Clearly, William Wrigley Jr. understood that, over the long term, a company cannot win at the expense of its business partners," Bill Wrigley said.

Wrigley knew the value of building loyalty and treated his employees like family. He started the five-day workweek in 1924, making him one of the first to give his employees Saturdays off. He also gave them medical care, life insurance and shares of stock.

Wrigley trusted his instincts enough to go against the crowd. Most of his rivals slashed costs during the depression of 1907. Wrigley seized the chance to advertise. Twice before, he'd spent $100,000 to launch ad campaigns in New York with few results. Still, he pumped $250,000 into a massive campaign during that depression. He was able to get billboard space cheaply, and the campaign proved successful.

Wrigley's Spearmint became the most popular brand of chewing gum by 1910.

"Tell 'em quick and tell 'em often" became his motto. During the 1920s, he placed cards promoting his gum in all 62,000 buses, subways and elevated train cars in the nation. Twice he sent four sticks of gum to every person in the phone book across the country.

It paid off. By 1922, the company was selling 10 billion sticks of gum a year.

Wrigley took a long-term view, aiming for the bigger pot of gold down the road. He invested at least $7 million in developing Catalina Island after buying it for $3.5 million in 1919.

"Profitability did not interfere with Wrigley's goals but rather was presumed to follow them at a distance," Fenster wrote. " 'Eventually,' he said of Catalina, 'I'll make up the cost by taking the smallest possible profit from an increased number of visitors.' "

Long View

Wrigley also held that the long-term view was best.

"I have sometimes been asked what single policy has been most profitable in our business, and I have always unhesitatingly answered, restraint in regard to immediate profits," Wrigley said in Fenster's book. "That has not only been our most profitable policy, it has been pretty nearly our only profitable one."

Wrigley also believed that innovation was crucial. As owner of the Cubs, he became one of the first in baseball to promote Ladies Day to bring women to the park.

He became the first owner to regularly broadcast his team's games live on the radio. Other owners feared radio would cause fans to stay home. Wrigley figured it would drum up interest and boost attendance. The Cubs broke the major league attendance record in 1929.

PART 3

Persevering Through Difficult Times

20

Organizer Nancy Brinker

Her Determination Helped
Foundation Spread The Word

Nancy Brinker thought about quitting as her cab pulled from a New York City curb one rainy day in 1982.

She'd just gotten out of a meeting with the president of a prominent lingerie company. The executive wanted nothing to do with Brinker's idea to put tags on underwear reminding buyers to get screened for breast cancer.

"She told me that it absolutely would not work, that her customers were thinking about beauty and glamour, not negative images like a disease," Brinker recalled. "I took it personally."

It wasn't the first or last door that was slammed in Brinker's face when she started her crusade to fight breast cancer.

"Breast cancer was like talking about death and taxes," Brinker said. "People weren't comfortable with it."

But Brinker didn't give up. She could still hear the words her older sister, Susan Komen, spoke before she died of breast cancer in 1980 at the age of 36.

"As soon as I get better, let's do something about this," Komen said. "You can find a way to speed up research; I know you can."

"When you promise somebody that you love to do something that they asked you to do, and they look at you in their final moments, I defy you not to do it," said Brinker, who at the time was an assistant buyer at department store chain Nieman Marcus. "I had to unleash a war on this disease."

Inspired To Action

The promise inspired Brinker. In 1982, two years after her sister's death, Brinker started the Susan G. Komen Foundation in Dallas. By 1999, the foundation had more than 35,000 volunteers nationwide and had raised more than $136 million. Its "Race for the Cure" is the largest series of 5-kilometer (3.1-mile) runs/fitness walks in the world. In the first two decades after its founding, the Komen Foundation awarded nearly 700 international research grants totaling more than $87 million.

Because of her work with the Komen Foundation, Brinker was named one of the "100 Most Important Women of the 20th Century" by *Ladies Home Journal* and one of *Biography* magazine's "25 Most Powerful Women in America." President George W. Bush appointed her as the U.S. ambassador to the Republic of Hungary in 2001.

Brinker realized early on that she had to sell her dream to make a difference. So she turned to her husband, Norman Brinker. She knew that as chairman and chief executive of Brinker International, Norman could advise her about her approach to corporations.

"He asked me to give him a bottom line," Brinker said. "I said, 'Look, the great tragedy of my young adulthood was the Vietnam war. We lost 59,000 Americans. In that same period, we lost 330,000 women to breast cancer.' It almost knocked him off his chair."

The statistics were a strong convincer. But to really grab people's attention, her husband said, Brinker should be armed with all the facts. "Norman always told me you have to refine and define a concept very well before you take it on the road. Seek to understand before you want to be understood," Brinker said.

So Brinker learned everything she could about breast cancer.

"I knew that if I expected people to reach into their pockets, I'd better learn a lot more about the disease scientifically. I studied with a vengeance. I called the National Cancer Institute and asked them to send me everything they could on the disease, and I read it."

Brinker started small. That way she saved money and had more time to define her mission. She set up shop in her guest bedroom with just a few hundred dollars, a shoebox full of names, a broken IBM typewriter and a volunteer secretary.

She knew she also needed others to help get the word out. So she called everyone she knew and asked them to lend a hand.

But then she had to start talking to people she didn't know. She realized that many people might be so turned off by the idea of cancer that they wouldn't listen to her.

Brinker analyzed the situation. How could she get people to focus on the battle against breast cancer?

She decided she had to make the effort fun. She'd launch a national series of 3.1-mile runs — short distances, so more people could participate. If people walked and ran, she reasoned, they'd be more willing to talk. If they were willing to talk, they'd be more open to learning about breast cancer.

"Everyone said it wouldn't work," said Brinker. "There was still the fear of the word 'cancer.' It was kind of like, wow, why don't you announce that you're going to have tax day?"

Brinker figured that if she could get big companies — household names — to sponsor the events, people would lose the fear. So she asked well-known companies such as American Airlines, Pier 1 Imports and JC Penney to back her.

Brinker went to corporate execs and urged them to think of their company's future. She used facts to show them that supporting her cause was good business. Breast cancer is the leading killer of women age 35 to 54, she told them. She challenged higher-ups to make sure the women in their workplace would have a future with the company, breast-cancer-free.

The plan worked. Companies forked over time, money, merchandise and ideas.

On a rainy Oct. 29, 1983, 800 people ran in the first Komen Race for the Cure. In 2002, a Race for the Cure was held in more than 100 U.S. cities and 3 foreign countries, with the number of expected participants exceeding 1.3 million.

Let Others Help

To be effective, Brinker says, you have to let people help you. Let them pour themselves into your dream and make it their own.

"It's amazing what you can get done if you don't care who gets the credit," she said. "You have to share the leadership, you have to be able to move away from some of the things you did every day and trust people in order to give people the ability to grow."

In 1984, Brinker had to rely on others when she herself was diagnosed with breast cancer at age 37. The treatment was painful, but Brinker survived by keeping her mind on her cause. She threw herself into her work and kept her calendar filled.

"I have always been a doer, always wanted to get things done yesterday. The long-term effect of having breast cancer for me has been to make me do everything in my life faster," she once wrote. "My chief role now is I panic at the right times. Even if that means meeting [with volunteers] at three in the morning."

Along with the Race for the Cure, the Komen Foundation raises money through other programs such as "Lee National Denim Day," Hallmark's "Cards for the Cure" and Sprint PCS' "Speak Out for Breast Cancer Awareness."

"People say to me, 'Did you know this was going to be so big?' I say, 'Yes, I did know this was going to be big. But I just didn't know what it was going to look like. You can't outline. You have to know in your heart that you have a vision, but you have to let the vision evolve.'"

21

Aviation Pioneer
William Boeing

In Building His Empire, He Bowed To
Just One Authority

The plaque William E. Boeing hung outside his office door said it all.

"There is no authority except facts. Facts are obtained by accurate observation. Deductions are to be made only from facts."

Strictly following that dictum, set down by the Greek physician Hippocrates, Boeing founded and built what became the world's largest maker of commercial aircraft, Chicago-based Boeing Co.

Boeing, a dropout from Yale University's school of engineering and the scion of a lumber family, wasn't the first to build airplanes commercially. But his close attention to fact and detail quickly propelled him to the top.

If the facts said something could be done, then Boeing refused to listen to any number of experts who said otherwise.

An example: About 10 years after starting to build airplanes, Boeing (1882–1956) concluded the company could profit carrying airmail for the United States Postal Service. He made that decision after examining a mass of detail on every possible objection.

Boeing put in a bid for the Chicago–San Francisco route, undercutting his rivals' bids by a third. His figures were so low, in fact, that the experts at other companies were sure he'd put himself out of business. Even the postal service doubted he could do the job and required the company to post a bond for the contract.

But his opponents weren't focused on one simple, obvious fact: The lighter the plane, the more mail it could carry. So he set a new standard by building lighter aircraft.

The move proved so profitable he quickly found a way to adapt his lighter planes to passenger traffic.

"My firm conviction from the start has been that science and hard work can lick what appear to be insurmountable difficulties," Boeing once said.

"I've tried to make the men around me feel, as I do, that we are embarked as pioneers upon a new science and industry in which our problems are so new and unusual that it behooves no one to dismiss any novel idea with the statement that 'it can't be done.' Our job is to keep everlastingly at research and experiment."

Boeing approached his hobbies in the same way. An avid fly fisherman, Boeing studied the habits of fish, built gadgets to help him tie better flies and experimented with new materials, such as polar bear hair, that might help him catch more fish.

Although Boeing immersed himself in his industry, learning to fly and setting up aviation clubs, he alone couldn't gather all the facts he needed. So he made sure that he had access to the best knowledge and science.

His engineers studied and corresponded with the best experts on aerodynamics and mechanics. Boeing partnered with the University of Washington to ensure his company hired trained people who were able to innovate.

During a severe downturn in the aircraft industry after World War I, Boeing kept key engineers on staff designing new and better planes — although there was no money to build them. Boeing risked his family's wealth to get projects off the ground.

An air show sparked his interest in planes when he was 28 years old and was building his own lumber fortune in the Seattle area. At the time, scientific elites pooh-poohed aviation, doubting it would ever amount to much more than an expensive joyride.

Boeing dismissed their doubts, especially after he had a chance to inspect a plane for the first time — and found right away that he and an engineer partner could improve it enough to make flying economical.

Friends implored Boeing to close during the recession after World War I. He'd begun paying the company's costs out of his own pocket.

Instead, he stuck with his certainty that aviation would succeed and turned to the manufacture of bedroom furniture and speedboats to stay afloat.

Boeing told a worker worried about the future of his job, "I'm prepared to run it like this . . . for another two years, and after those two years, we will never look back."

But having the facts support his vision was only part of Boeing's formula for success.

He also demanded perfection. It was said that not even the fish Boeing tried to catch saw him unshaven.

Boeing often went into his factory to watch people work. Workers responsible for flaws and less-than-conscientious work met with consequences. Boeing summarily fired a worker who was responsible for frayed cables on a model he was trying to sell the Navy.

In another instance, a worker used wood that had accidentally been nicked and told Boeing it would be good enough. Boeing destroyed the wood as the workers looked on.

At the same time, Boeing realized that his workers were not to blame for the fact that his vision would take a long time to realize.

"He was willing to sink any number of 'dry wells' if he thought he was drilling in the right field," an associate once said. "If he believed you were moving in the direction of progress, he would support you all the way in spite of temporary failures."

22

AmeriCredit's
Michael Barrington

Attitude Put Him In Driver's Seat Of

Auto Loan Titan

When Michael R. Barrington wanted his senior staff to get a message, he didn't just sit them down in a meeting.

Instead, the former chief executive and president of AmeriCredit Corp. once marched his 100 top managers from the firm's Fort Worth, Texas, headquarters to a nearby movie theater to create a conversation about company culture.

With the group seated and the lights dimmed, the movie *Remember the Titans* began to roll. The true story about the 1971 Alexandria, Va., high school football team — the Titans — showed a racially diverse group triumph through teamwork and mutual respect. Afterward, the group of managers discussed the movie.

"When I went to see the movie myself just for entertainment, I was amazed at the parallels to our culture at AmeriCredit," Barrington said. "The movie sends a powerful message about how diverse people can come together and accomplish more as a team."

That strategy is one of the many ways he shaped 3,500 employees into a Titanlike team. Together they grabbed leadership in the market of subprime auto loans, funding buyers with less-than-perfect credit history.

Other company CEOs might want to pop over to their neighborhood video store. Indeed, in 2000, a year in which the Federal

Reserve made life difficult for moneylenders by raising interest rates six times, AmeriCredit was nevertheless able to turn in a stellar performance.

Sales at the Texas firm soared from $80 million in 1996 to $510 million in 2000. The company's 2000 figure represented a 50% increase from the previous year. Earnings shot from 34 cents a share to $1.59 in the same period.

In 2000, the $200 billion market segment included about one in five car buyers. AmeriCredit ended that year with an $8.2 billion loan portfolio, writing about 30,000 loans a month.

Michael Barrington helped put AmeriCredit on top. Named CEO in July 2000, he was the go-to guy since being made chief operating officer and president in 1995.

Barrington brought to the table a wealth of business experience from his steady climb through the ranks, from financial analyst to bank loan officer to manager to chief executive.

At AmeriCredit's creation in 1992, Barrington's business instincts of what works and what doesn't were right on target because they were drawn from his successes as well as from a bad crash and burn.

Barrington also brought an attitude — that of success. "I learned at a very early age to never accept a problem," Barrington said. "I always treat it like a challenge, something that can be overcome with enough work and thought. My overriding theme would be that I am in constant pursuit of the next right thing."

He worked tirelessly to bring his diverse employees together, putting to use the lessons of his 20+ years in business and working his family's farm.

"Leave egos at the door," Barrington said, "They have no place here. We champion teamwork."

He set high standards at AmeriCredit. "I'm pretty much never satisfied with the status quo," Barrington said. "I always believe we can do better. I have been described as having loyalty to execution. I think that means I'm very focused on the execution of our business."

He foremost valued his team. Asked about his success, he inevitably shifted the focus to his employees. They got most of his attention.

In January 2001, the then-41-year-old executive personally met with all 1,500 of his Fort Worth call center workers in three one-day sessions. He spoke with all of them, thanking each individually. He returned to headquarters from a lengthy question-and-answer period loaded with feedback. Work shift flexibility and family health medical coverage came up repeatedly, and management set about addressing those issues.

"I committed to those employees that every question asked will get an answer," Barrington said. "That means we're assessing every idea offered, whether it's something we could do."

Barrington's business basics were learned as a fourth-grader working on his family's dairy farm in Okemah, Okla. The family's 200 chickens produced a whole lot of eggs. Too young to drive, the little entrepreneur invested in a 1964 Volkswagen Beetle and got his mother to drive him around town. He landed accounts selling eggs to many of the town's restaurants and 2,000 residents.

After graduating with a bachelor's degree in agricultural economics from Oklahoma State University in 1980, Barrington went to work for Gulf Oil Corp. as a budget and planning operations manager. There he learned the fickleness of a marketplace. The oil industry was booming when he started, but five years later, when he left, it had gone bust. "You can never take success for granted," Barrington said.

In late 1984, Barrington joined a predecessor of what is today Bank One Corp. As a loan officer, he learned to evaluate credit worthiness of companies. "When you do a credit analysis at a bank, you get pretty darn good at understanding balance sheets and income statements and how capital is formed," Barrington said. "I can't think of many life experiences that would teach you more about the need to be accurate. A lot is riding on the analysis you do."

In 1989, Barrington left the bank as a senior vice president to join a little start-up called Urcarco Inc., a used-car seller. It was soon in deep financial trouble and became, he said, "one of the defining moments in the life of Mike Barrington."

It was an impossible logistics dance of buying and selling massive quantities of used cars with no statistical safeguards that could show who was a good credit risk. The fiasco left Barrington with what he calls "a great sense of failure. That [failure] took me a time to get through. It's also the most valuable experience I've ever had. It caused me to [learn] the importance of [testing] everything before you try to do it."

Although he couldn't see it at the time, Urcarco's failure provided the map for AmeriCredit's success. The solution was in an innovation that Barrington calls "data mining."

More information about applicants would surely help make better lending decisions, he figured. From its very first loan, AmeriCredit gathered information from each loan application into a massive database.

Software was created to measure the data that could then predict, with uncanny accuracy, the extent of a new applicant's credit risk. "No competitor has the amount of data we have available on this profile of the population," Barrington said.

Barrington also pushed AmeriCredit employees to focus on customers' needs. The company conducts an annual survey of its auto dealership customers, listening for their needs. One year, speed of loan financing turned up on the survey. At that time, a loan took four business days to fund. Barrington decided it needed to be done faster.

So he made sure new database technology was brought onboard. Soon, 95% of the firm's loans were made in less than 24 hours.

Barrington said he continues to learn by looking beyond one's first quick opinion about an idea.

"Many of life's greatest opportunities lie behind the easy presumption that something won't work," he said.

23

Nvidia's Jen-Hsun Huang
His Laserlike Focus Helps Keep His Company On Top

For Jen-Hsun Huang, the issue is never price. It's quality.

After trying to sell chips to companies and failing, Nvidia was ready to go out of business. Nvidia co-founder Chris Malchowsky recalls that Chief Executive Jen-Hsun Huang took what at the time seemed to be odd steps to try and save the company.

"What he directed us to do is go build the best product we could build. He said, 'Don't worry about the size of the chip.' He said, 'Get it out on time and make it as fast as you can,'" Malchowsky said. Most rivals at the time were trying to build chips as small and cheaply as possible, figuring they had to slash prices to beat the competition.

"Jen-Hsun recognized if we could provide a significantly better mousetrap — better, faster and more capable — we would be able to get value out of it. And we'd only be able to do that if the chip was good."

So the company scrapped 2½ years of development and went to work on a new design. It launched the new chip, called Riva, in April 1997. The device finally brought the company success.

Nvidia was one of the best-performing chip companies in 2001, which was one of the worst years up to that time in the history of the semiconductor industry.

In the first quarter of 2001, its sales grew 62% year over year to $241 million. It completed the purchase of rival 3dfx Interactive and began shipping its first graphic chips to a new customer, Apple Computer Inc.

Every major maker of video game boxes uses Nvidia chips. And as of 2001 — less than 10 years after Nvidia's 1993 incorporation — one out of every three personal computers shipped had a Nvidia processor inside.

The company's success came largely because Huang chose to build high-quality chips rather than sell on price alone. His gamble paid off. But he says back in 1996 when the company was on the line, he was scared.

"There was certainly a sense of fear. The fear was not of going out of business or anything like that. The fear was really about letting people down," Huang said. He used that fear to focus on what needed to be done.

Once he figured that out, he never veered from his course. "You have to select your target extraordinarily well. And pick one or two things to go do; don't pick 10 things to go do," he said.

When Nvidia had its near-death experience, all petty arguing went out the window, Huang says. In situations like that, he says, nothing matters but survival.

To keep that energy, Huang tells himself and his employees to think like the company is going to go out of business in 30 days unless they do what needs to be done.

Huang was born in Taipei, Taiwan to parents who were well educated but of modest means. He remembers the main transportation the family had was a motor scooter. At times, he and his parents and his two brothers would all pile onto the scooter to get around.

Huang's father tutored at a local college part time and worked part time as an engineer. His parents taught him that work is a natural part of life, to be enjoyed rather than dreaded.

"I don't feel like I'm working when I'm working," Huang said. "It's just what I do. I like what I do. You don't complain about work, and you don't get tired from working."

His father had visited the U.S. while on assignment for Carrier Corp., an air conditioning company. He came back to Taiwan with a goal for his family.

"All I remember is my father saying that it was an amazing country and we should go some day. And from that day on, he wanted to make sure we would grow up and have the United States be a land of opportunity for us," Huang said.

To prepare their children for the move, Huang's mother taught them English at an early age.

"We learned the A, B, Cs when I was about 6," Huang said. "My mother, who to this day can't speak English, would pick out 10 words in Webster's *English Dictionary* and ask us what it meant in Chinese every single day."

When he was 7, the family moved to Thailand. When the government there became unstable, his parents sent Huang and his older brother to the U.S. He was 10 at the time, and his brother was 11½.

An uncle met them at an airport in Tacoma, Wash. He immediately put the boys into a boarding school in Oneida, Ky. They stayed there for a year and a half before their parents came to the U.S., and the family settled in Oregon. The uncle had unwittingly put the boys into a reform school for juvenile delinquents.

"If you want to teach a kid to overcome fear, send them to Oneida, Kentucky," Huang said.

He was the youngest student in a school of 600 students, half boys and half girls. He says he and his brother were the first Chinese that school had ever seen.

"I cleaned up all the dorms for the rest of the kids every day after school. It taught my brother and me how to be independent, how to take care of ourselves," Huang said.

There might've been prejudice, but he didn't notice it. "It turned out everybody was very gracious," he said. "Whatever meanness they had, we were too young to pick up. I think our age, our naiveness and our innocence toward the whole place made it possible for us to survive."

Having a positive attitude enabled him not only to survive but also to thrive in his new homeland.

Huang was also too busy to feel sorry for himself. He'd learned pingpong at a young age, and at 16, he became a nationally rated champion.

Like his father, he was interested in engineering. Huang went to Oregon State University, where he earned a bachelor's degree in electrical engineering. He went on to earn a master's degree in engineering from Stanford University.

Realizing he wanted to help spur the cutting edge, Huang went to work at network computer maker Sun Microsystems Inc. in Mountain View, Calif. There he met Chris Malchowsky and Curtis

Priem, and the trio founded Nvidia Corp. in 1993. They set out to make graphics chips for PCs and video game machines.

After that first big stumble in 1996, Nvidia refocused on its core business and didn't look back. In January 1999, Nvidia came public at $9.50 a share. Two years later it soared to more than $90.

In early 2003, the stock was back down to $12. Still, Nvidia's revenue grew 50% in 2002, a leader in its market.

Huang said he was having a lot more fun in those golden-stock days than when Nvidia had its back to the wall. But he knows better than to let up when times are good.

"The stuff that I've found extraordinarily difficult is hiring the best of the best, convincing them to come to your company so you can fulfill your vision," he said.

Hiring the best people was especially challenging in the early days when he was a 30-year-old chief executive. He overcame this by focusing on selling himself and his company.

"You're selling to your customers, you're selling to your investors and you're selling to your employees," he said. "You have to show them there's an opportunity here."

Huang knows that learning is a lifelong process. That applies especially to customer relations. "I call on our customers as frequently as I'm allowed to," he said. "I love seeing customers. I learn something new every time.

"There's no question I come home with a new strategy every time I see a customer. In the final analysis, you're here because you're solving problems for your customers."

24

Entrepreneur Daisy Braxton
How She Used Her Fall Into Welfare
To Reach Higher Than She Ever Had

Daisy Braxton's life went into a tailspin in 1989 when Sears, undergoing a major downsizing, cut her full-time sales position.

To feed her five children, Braxton, a single mother, took odd jobs at fast-food restaurants in her hometown of Newport News, Va. Not only were they minimum-wage jobs, but they also offered no health benefits, she recalled.

To make matters worse, her children began getting sick and having dental problems one after the other. Unable to keep up with the doctors' bills, she took a step that she dreaded: She applied for welfare.

That move could have led to lifelong dependency. But Braxton refused to fall into that trap. Instead, she took steps to climb higher than she ever had. She started by volunteering for a training course in janitorial work. Job training is now a requirement for most welfare recipients under welfare reform.

"I think that welfare reform is probably one of the best things to happen in this country," the then-43-year-old Braxton said in 1999. "It gives people an opportunity to rise to the occasion and provide for themselves, as they should have all along."

In 1992, she started Superior Janitorial Services Inc. with two employees. In her first year, she had $45,000 in sales. By 1995, she was up to $60,000. Three years later, she topped $260,000. By 2000, she'd expanded to 18 employees.

Commitment To Quality

Braxton started her business after two years of working for other commercial janitors and doing residential cleaning on the side. Her first step in starting Superior Janitorial was to vow to herself that her firm would do a top-quality job. And it did, consistently.

That led to a series of opportunities. Word got around that she was reliable, and the Newport News Housing Authority, where she'd trained, asked her to return as an instructor. While there, Braxton heard about an opportunity to clean apartments in the NNHA's senior-citizen housing complexes. Her sound reputation helped her land the deal.

She hired six workers and was put in charge of cleaning 24 buildings. Her performance there generated more referrals. Building on her success, she got the contract to clean transient housing for the Army and Navy.

To ensure quality didn't suffer as she expanded, Braxton established standard cleaning procedures — her employees follow the dusty trail from light fixtures to carpet, room by room, building by building.

She also set up a supervisory system. When the workers were done, supervisors checked everything from trash removal to disinfection of bathrooms.

The system worked, and her strategy paid off. Satisfied customers spread the word, and she began to land deals in the private sector.

"The work they do is excellent," said Gayle Major, project manager for American Mansions Corp., a real estate management company with which Braxton contracts.

If there's a problem, Braxton takes steps to correct it immediately. "She makes sure that everybody is well-trained, and if we do have a problem, she is right on it," Major said.

Most of Braxton's hires come from the welfare rolls. Recently, she acquired a contract to clean a drug rehabilitation center and hired several of the program's recovering addicts. She's more interested in potential than history, she says.

"I look for a teachable spirit," she said. "I can motivate people, but they have to start with a little spark."

Braxton's system helps her quickly weed out people who aren't reliable. If people show up on time and follow her checklist, it's a good indication they can be trained to do a high-quality job.

Under her system, she requires workers to get themselves to "Point A" in the morning. She then coordinates the company's two vans to move people to "Points B, C and D" throughout the day.

Although word of mouth has been her greatest source of clients, Braxton is always on the lookout for new business. She scans the papers every day for requests for proposals on cleaning jobs and applies for everything that she thinks is feasible. She'll take on almost any job, no matter how small.

"I have to be out there looking aggressively all the time," Braxton said. "People and businesses move, so you have to constantly be on the lookout for new work."

Braxton listens carefully to clients and remains sensitive to their needs, as well as those of her workers. For example, before assigning a former addict or someone who has spent time in jail to a job, she'll make sure the client is comfortable with the proposed arrangement.

Close Eye

She also makes sure there's nothing in the customer's place of business that might tempt such workers, assigning them mostly to clean empty buildings for new tenants. She keeps a close eye on them when they're starting out.

Braxton urges her workers to come to "understand my way of thinking," she said. She encourages them to take on added responsibility and exploit the opportunities the company provides, including booking steady work and gaining management experience.

She sets her goals to exceed the client's and expects her employees to rise to the occasion. She'll clean nooks and crannies that the client forgot he had. And she does windows. Happily.

It's that focus on detail that leaves her customers feeling and looking good. "We are a small business ourselves," Major said. "Daisy's success has been an important part of our success as well."

25

IGT's Charles Mathewson
Relationship-Building
Helped Him Win Big

Charles Mathewson didn't really read fiction. He liked the real
stuff. And his favorite types of books from age 10 on usually had
something to do with stocks and financial markets.

He soaked up all the information he could before he plunged
into the business world. With that kind of jump-start, Mathewson
found financial success early. He followed that up by stepping into
the boardroom to turn a struggling slot-machine maker into a world
powerhouse.

Mathewson is chairman of International Game Technology Inc.,
the world's largest maker of computerized gaming machines.

"The inner workings of financial markets have always fascinated
me," the then-73-year-old executive said in 2001. "I always wanted
to make money using my brains. But in truth, it takes a lot of hard
work to make what you know turn out as a reality."

To learn about finance from the inside out, Mathewson worked
seven days a week, first as a clerk and then as a broker. He was so
good at it that before reaching age 40 he was financially set to retire.

"He's a voracious reader with an obvious passion for what he
does," said longtime friend and former IGT executive Bud Russell,
who's known Mathewson since both were high school students in
Long Beach, Calif. "He's a big-picture type of guy who can talk
about almost any topic. And that brings him into contact with all
sorts of people."

Mathewson believes perseverance is key to any endeavor, no matter how many times someone else says "No."

He remembers one of his early customers was a University of Southern California professor. He met him while trying to get into upper-division classes. At first, the professor rejected him for lacking the proper prerequisite lower-division course work.

But Mathewson refused to take that "No." He talked with the instructor day after day, pleading his case.

His determination persuaded the professor to reverse his decision.

He wound up performing well enough to keep taking more upper-level courses. His stick-to-itiveness so impressed the instructor that he became the man's stockbroker following graduation.

Mathewson knows success is built on relationships and works overtime to make sure he forges good ones.

"He has a wonderful sense of the importance of keeping in touch with people," said Russell. "He carries a massive phone book with him, and he really works at remembering people's names. It certainly has helped him build contacts and get to know people on both a professional as well as a business level."

Some of those contacts include powerful movers in the business world. He shares a passion for bridge with Warren Buffett, his friend for some four decades.

Actually, Mathewson isn't averse to mixing business with pleasure. It's all part of his reach for balance in his life.

"Work and play aren't separate parts of my life — what I do for a living is something that's also very enjoyable to me," said Mathewson. "I don't know how many times I've been at a dinner and someone will say something that gives me an investment idea. Success is a concept that has to be with you every part of every day."

One of his early leads led to a friendship with another up-and-coming broker, Boyd Jefferies. Both operated from a southern California base. When Jefferies decided to start his own company in 1962, Mathewson signed on and quickly became Jefferies & Co.'s No. 2 shareholder. Seven years later, Jefferies & Co. had become a hot property among larger, more established financial firms. In 1969, the company was sold for $50 million to Investors Diversified Services Inc.

"Back in those days, that was a lot of money," said Mathewson. "It certainly gave me enough to live comfortably on for the rest of my life."

But looking after his own portfolio, which included several smaller companies he'd invested heavily in, just wasn't enough. Always up for a challenge, Mathewson noticed IGT.

He liked its products and bought 80,000 shares of stock in the small gaming machine manufacturer in the early 1980s.

A few years later, he met the firm's chairman, Si Redd. The two became friends, and Redd started talking to Mathewson about IGT's difficulties in expanding. Eventually Redd coaxed Mathewson into taking a more active role in the company.

In 1986, IGT was stumbling, and Redd enlisted Mathewson to take over full-time.

Knowing he'd need help, Mathewson started hiring experts he'd admired. Soon, IGT was back in the black, and its profits were rising.

By the early 1990s, IGT was sailing. It had taken a dominant position in the industry. So Mathewson retired from daily operations as chief executive. But new leadership came in with big plans to go in different directions.

Then came trouble. An economic slowdown and resistance to some of the new plans by several senior managers slowed IGT's growth, says Reed Bingham, a longtime friend whom Mathewson added to IGT's management roster. Many key executives left.

"Six of our top people left, mad at the direction the company was taking," Bingham said. "They got new jobs and were set when Chuck decided he had to come out of retirement again."

Believing the company needed to recoup the sense of teamwork it once had, Mathewson resumed daily control of IGT in 1995. "The first thing he did was to convince everyone who had left to come back," he said. "They all had found very good positions with solid companies. But they just picked up and left because Chuck needed their help."

His plan worked. Mathewson helped push annual earnings per share up from 92 cents in 1996 to $1.77 in 2000.

Just because he values relationships doesn't mean Mathewson is a soft touch. When he has to make a tough decision, he approaches it head-on. Yet he makes sure the people he's dealing with know he respects them.

"He's the only guy I know who can fire an executive and take him out to lunch the next day and still be friends," Bingham laughed.

Mathewson tries mightily to understand the role each person plays in the company. He analyzes each person's talents and searches for the right place for them.

Mathewson says that he strived to create an atmosphere at IGT where employees at every level were willing to take chances. "You've got to be wrong a certain amount of the time before you can expect to be successful," he said. "I know I've certainly made my share of mistakes. Learning from those mistakes is one of the greatest foundations I've found to teach me how to invest smarter."

In late 2000, with IGT's future seemingly secure, Mathewson removed himself from day-to-day affairs of corporate life. But he remained as chairman, in his office almost every day.

And few expect Mathewson to bring up the "r" word anytime soon. "What I've learned is that money is something you've got to have to keep a roof over your head," he said. "But it really doesn't matter. The important thing is to make a living doing something you can have fun doing."

That's a lesson he's tried to drill into his employees. It's also something he's taken to heart in bringing up his five children.

"I've had to be careful, because I never want to deny them the right to struggle," said Mathewson. "You can give someone too much help. In the end, that can stifle a person's growth and keep them from learning to stand on their own."

26

Tellabs' Michael Birck

Brashness Got Him Started, Tempering It Moved Him Up

Impetuous. Unable to think things through. Jumps in without weighing the pros and cons.

They're not qualities you'd put at the top of your résumé. But they're all characteristics of the chief executive and co-founder of Tellabs Inc., an international maker of communications systems that raised annual earnings an average of 76% from 1992 to 1997 and met its "2B by 2K" ($2 billion in sales by 2000) a year ahead of schedule. Those traits gave Michael Birck the gumption to start his own business in 1975 at age 37.

At the same time, he recognized that those very traits would have to be tempered to sustain his Lisle, Ill.–based corporation, which managed to operate in the black during the economic downturn of the early 2000s when other telecom-related companies went bust.

The combination of passion and purpose has driven Birck a long way from the central Indiana farm where he grew up, the eldest son in a family of five.

He developed a lot of technical skills growing up. He'd pick up clocks, watches and other gizmos, take them apart and put them back together again. He says he inherited that aptitude from his father, a mail carrier, whom he idolized.

"I learned everything from him," Birck said. "My father would have been a superb mechanical engineer."

Instead, his father got trapped in a rigid job in the U.S. Postal Service. And that had a profound effect on young Michael. Seeing his father's constant frustration fueled an entrepreneurial spirit and strong distaste for bureaucracy.

"Though I didn't know what its name was, my dad complained a lot about the regimentation of the post office, and I knew [bureaucracy] wasn't conducive to people doing their best," Birck said. "I saw him trapped within that."

As a youngster and teen-ager, he went to a "little red schoolhouse" where he excelled in math and science. His teacher gave him a lot of one-on-one attention, which, in turn, inspired Birck to go to college. He was the only one of the 11 students in his class to do so.

But in his first semester at Purdue University in West Lafayette, Ind., Birck thought he was way out of his league at a big university. Not only were his studies more difficult than he expected, but culture shock also overwhelmed him. By Thanksgiving, he was convinced he'd earn only average grades and lose his scholarship.

"I had to make the honor roll to keep it. I thought there was no way I [could] make it," he recalled.

He did, but just barely. Birck got mostly Bs and one A. But more importantly, clearing that seemingly insurmountable hurdle gave him the confidence he needed to pursue the rest of his schooling and, later, his career.

From the outset, Birck rebelled against constraints at work. His early memories of bureaucracy's stale legacy in his family resurfaced when he started work at Bell Telephone Laboratories in 1960. At the same time, he began studying for his master's degree in electrical engineering.

Birck desperately wanted to develop systems for Bell but got stuck writing system requirements for others to develop. He asked to be transferred, but management refused.

Experiencing firsthand the frustration that stymied his father, Birck vowed he'd eventually start a company filled with entrepreneurial fire. He left Bell and, over the next 14 years, worked on product development at Continental Telephone and moved into management at Wescom Inc., another telecommunications company.

At all three companies, he built capital to start his own firm by joining the employee stock plan or getting a stake in the firm as part of his compensation.

In 1975, Birck left Wescom and risked his savings by launching Tellabs with two colleagues. He jumped in headfirst. But brashness would cost him dearly early on.

Birck admits that in his zeal to expand the company, he gave the green light on developing a long-distance routing system, the Titan 5500 series, without having adequately assessed the project.

That mistake cost the company years of bad publicity as well as five times as much money as originally planned to keep the project afloat.

Throughout those bleak years, when analysts were pronouncing Titan dead on arrival, Birck says that he never lost faith. He kept morale from plummeting with pep talks and a keen sense of humor, says John Foulkes, a member of Tellabs' board. Birck often joked that the Titan could spell disaster. It was, after all, just two letters away from spelling Titanic.

But the Titan 5500 would eventually develop into the company's flagship product. Sales of the series jumped 69% in 1996.

Foulkes says Birck developed a firm grip on what's possible in the ever-changing world of technology.

"He's about as proud as an old shoe, so he doesn't have any enlarged ideas," Foulkes said. "He's not super-intelligent, but he can spot the value in ideas and where things are at the moment. . . . His engineers could never pull the wool over his eyes."

William Souders, another board member, agrees.

"Mike is a very interesting combination of technological expertise and business acumen," he said. "He is as interested in the bottom line, inventories and margins as he is the latest technology."

When spotting new technology, Birck is now careful to temper initial enthusiasm. To help develop perspective, he'll go running or play tennis or golf.

"Impetuousness and not being thorough in thinking through things before embarking on them [are my weaknesses]," he said. "In an entrepreneur, that can be a modest strength, if it's not exercised to a fault."

To ward against that, he'll hire people who are more methodical than he is. And several times, his lieutenants have pulled his finger off the trigger.

How does he find the right people?

He looks for risk-takers with a plan and an ability to rein in a chief executive.

27

Electronics Maker
Konosuke Matsushita
His Focus On Vision Boosted
Him To The Top

In 1932, Konosuke Matsushita summoned the 1,100 workers from his fast-growing Japanese electronics company for a meeting. Many of those at the Osaka Central Electric Club Auditorium that spring morning expected to hear praise for their skillful work and high-quality products.

But Matsushita knew that those elements weren't enough for his maturing company anymore. The firm had to keep striving to be the best.

So he threw down an awesome challenge.

"The mission of a manufacturer is to overcome poverty, to relieve society as a whole from misery and bring it wealth," Matsushita declared. "Beginning today, this far-reaching dream, this sacred calling, will be our ideal and our mission, and its fulfillment the responsibility of each one of us."

By laying out a vision and working toward it in all he did, Matsushita (1894–1989) turned his young electronics firm into one of the world's greatest companies. Ten years after his death, Osaka-based Matsushita Electric Industrial Co. had $64 billion in annual sales and was the world's largest consumer electronics maker. Its brands include Panasonic, Quasar, National, Technics and JVC.

"Konosuke believed that without a sound business philosophy, a company would lose its way in this highly competitive world," said

Masaharu Matsushita, the founder's son-in-law, who served as president and, later, chairman of the company. (Matsushita had no sons, so Masaharu adopted his last name upon marrying his daughter.) "It is only after the philosophical groundwork has been laid that the employees, technology and capital of a company can be utilized to the best advantage."

Matsushita drafted seven principles to guide him and his workers. They include public service, teamwork and tirelessly striving for progress. The resulting sense of shared purpose is one of Matsushita Electric's greatest competitive edges.

How did Matsushita get others to buy into his vision?

He made sure he communicated his ideas clearly. For years, Matsushita directed workers to read the company's principles aloud each morning. In 1935, he drafted a pamphlet outlining Matsushita Electric's mission for shop owners selling its products. For managers, he wrote parables about each principle.

"He had a way of taking these principles and introducing them to you in the form of short, easy-to-understand stories," said Richard Kraft, a retired president of Matsushita Electric's U.S. unit who worked with the company's founder from 1974 to 1989.

To make sure his employees shared his goals, Matsushita got them involved. In 1933, he set up a division system to pass his outlook on to younger managers. Each unit handled production, sales and profits. Managers paid their own bills with no help from corporate headquarters.

From incoming graduates to factory workers, Matsushita educated his staff in his philosophy. In the mid-1930s, he opened two training centers to teach business skills and convey his ideals. Students spent four hours a day studying and the rest of their time in offices, factories and shops.

"All the training programs, even if they were trying to make you a better assembler, stuck in something on the principles," said John P. Kotter, author of *Matsushita Leadership* and the Konosuke Matsushita Professor of Leadership at Harvard Business School.

"We are a company of many presidents — that's what he used to say," Kraft recalled.

Matsushita wanted to keep employees from getting complacent. So he stressed humility.

As his company grew and managers demanded bigger budgets, Matsushita hung pictures of Thomas Edison on office walls and erected a statue of the inventor on the company grounds. They were a reminder: Edison, who made great contributions to society, once supported his research by selling newspapers.

Matsushita led by example. In 1935, he asked a plant manager to join him on visits to retailers. As the two made rounds, Matsushita presented himself and his cards to everyone he met — from store executives to shop ladies waiting on customers. To the most junior store clerk, he bowed humbly — an unheard-of gesture for a top Japanese executive.

"No matter how large Matsushita Electric might become, never forget to maintain the modest attitude of a merchant," he said. "Think of yourselves as being employed in a small store, and carry out your work with simplicity, frugality and humility."

Matsushita didn't tolerate loss. Profit is a reward for constantly raising efficiency and reducing costs, he said. Making money is a company's obligation to society, he believed.

"If we cannot make a good profit, we are committing a sort of crime against society," Matsushita told his managers. "We take society's capital, people and materials, yet without a good profit, we are using precious resources that could be better used elsewhere."

In the early 1980s, Kraft went to Japan to inform Matsushita of losses at the Quasar television unit. Matsushita, who suffered from health problems all his life, sat at a desk in his hospital room. He was enraged at the news.

"I thought he was going to be back in bed again," Kraft said.

But Matsushita tried to focus on the positive. He coached Kraft on how to fix the troubles at Quasar, which Matsushita Electric had bought from Motorola Inc. in 1974. Upgrade production lines, cut costs and outsource some assembly, Matsushita told him.

"I never saw him criticize someone in a way that wasn't constructive," Kraft said. "The Matsushita management style turned around the operation."

Matsushita relished constructive criticism. After once reprimanding a junior executive, he told the executive he was lucky to have someone to criticize him.

"If I made such a mistake," Matsushita said, "there is no one who would say anything right to me, but you bet there would be a lot of criticism behind my back. And that doesn't help."

When Matsushita did face criticism, he looked at it objectively and sought to find his role in the problem.

In 1964, Matsushita gathered 167 wholesalers at a resort near Tokyo. Japan's economy was in a slump, and the wholesalers were reeling. They groused to Matsushita, blaming him for their woes. Matsushita's first response was that the wholesalers' problems were their own. Tempers flared.

But Matsushita then thought about the grievances more carefully. He realized some of the complaints about his company might be justified. If a product didn't sell well, it was as much his problem as that of his wholesalers. So he addressed the group again.

"My assertion that you are not managing your companies well was thoughtless, and a grave error on my part," he told the group. "As of today, Matsushita Electric will make some basic changes in its sales programs."

Matsushita believed that mistakes and setbacks are chances to learn and improve.

One of Matsushita's greatest lessons stemmed from World War II. Japan's military rulers enlisted him to make bayonets, ships and planes. Facing the loss of his company, Matsushita had no choice but to go along.

The war devastated Matsushita's business. Still, he refused to focus on the failure or the company's manufacture of munitions. Instead, he spent the next decade rebuilding his company and, through his products, the nation.

"He walked away from World War II thinking the entire episode was insane," Kotter said. "A lot of his later life was aimed at peace in the greater sense."

In 1946, Matsushita started the PHP Institute, a think tank dedicated to peace and happiness through prosperity. One of the aims was to keep Japan from going to war again. Out of disgust for the politicians who led Japan into war, Matsushita in 1979 started the Matsushita Institute of Government and Management near Tokyo for aspiring leaders. In less than 20 years, according to Kotter, an impressive 10% of MIGM's alumni were members of the Japanese legislature.

28

Ebony's John H. Johnson

How He Went From A Tin-Roof Shack To The Forbes 400

It was 1942, and John H. Johnson needed a $500 loan to start his first magazine, *Negro Digest*. "Boy," said the loan officer at a Chicago bank, "we don't make any loans to colored people."

The 24-year-old Johnson felt his anger rise. But in that instant, he recalled the advice of Dale Carnegie and other self-improvement authors he'd been reading since he was a teen-ager.

"Don't get mad," he thought to himself. "Get smart."

He queried the loan officer about who did lend to blacks, Johnson recalled in his autobiography, *Succeeding Against the Odds*.

The loan officer answered that the only place he knew was Citizens Loan Corp., a finance company. Johnson asked the loan officer for the name of a contact there and whether he could cite him as a reference.

With renewed interest and apparent bewilderment, the official replied, "Of course," Johnson wrote.

Born in a tin-roof shack in Arkansas, Johnson was on his way to becoming the first black American on the *Forbes* magazine list of the 400 richest people in the U.S. Using his mother's furniture as collateral, he got his loan and launched Johnson Publishing Co.

His *Ebony* magazine, with a paid circulation exceeding 1.75 million in 2001, has been the No. 1 black-oriented magazine for more than 50 years. *Jet,* aimed at a younger audience, had a 2001 paid circulation of nearly 1 million.

Privately held Johnson Publishing, which employed 2,600 people in 1998, also owns Fashion Fair cosmetics, the No. 1 line of cosmetics for black women. It's sold in more than 2,500 stores worldwide.

Johnson credits much of his success to his mother. Providing loan collateral was just one of many sacrifices she made for her son. Working as a domestic, she saved money to move to Chicago when he was a teen-ager, so he'd have greater opportunity.

"Because my mother made such great sacrifices for me, I didn't just want to succeed for myself. I wanted to succeed for her," Johnson said in an interview.

When he moved to Chicago at the age of 15, Johnson's high school classmates poked fun at his southern drawl and "mammy-made clothes."

But he learned to deal with adversity by heading to the library and reading self-help books and the biographies of successful people. Dale Carnegie's *How to Win Friends and Influence People* particularly impressed him.

"What Dale Carnegie said is that you shouldn't be preoccupied with unpleasant things. You ought to always try to look on the brighter side of things, to do the things you can do, and not worry about the things you cannot do," Johnson noted. "I read that book 50 times, and it helped me."

Johnson said Carnegie gave him the confidence to speak up. His classmates' scorn, he said, turned to respect. They elected him president of the junior and senior classes.

After high school, Johnson got an education in business basics by working as an assistant to Harry Pace, founder and chief executive of Supreme Liberty Life Insurance Co., one of the largest black businesses in America.

Pace and other executives taught him to "size up a situation and determine if it advanced my interests" and, if it did, to "focus all my energies on that one point," he wrote.

Take how he increased circulation at *Negro Digest*. Aiming for the top, he asked first lady Eleanor Roosevelt to write an article for the column, "If I Were a Negro." Roosevelt initially answered that she'd love to but didn't have time.

That wasn't a flat-out no, he noted, so he continued correspondence. When she was in Chicago, he sent her a telegram, asking if she'd have a few minutes to dictate a column.

That worked. Roosevelt's piece, saying she'd not only have great bitterness if she were black but also great patience, caused a sensation. Almost overnight, *Negro Digest's* circulation nearly doubled to 100,000.

An even bigger challenge was finding a major company that would advertise regularly in *Ebony*, which Johnson launched in 1945. He set his sights on Zenith Radio Co. and its CEO, Eugene McDonald, in 1947.

The executive agreed to a meeting but warned Johnson that "if you try to talk to me about putting an ad in your publication, I will end the interview."

Johnson looked up McDonald in *Who's Who in America*, as he does everyone he meets for the first time.

"I want to know where they came from, what are their interests, what can I talk to them about. You have to establish rapport with people, and you establish rapport by having mutual interests and mutual knowledge of each other."

Reading that McDonald was an arctic explorer, Johnson called Matthew Henson, the black assistant to Adm. Robert Peary, who was recognized as leader of the first expedition to reach the North Pole.

He had Henson autograph his autobiography for McDonald. He also assigned a story on Henson for *Ebony*.

When Johnson presented McDonald with the autographed book and article and explained that the magazine tried to highlight black successes, McDonald nodded his head, and said, "You know, I don't see any reason why we shouldn't advertise in this magazine."

Carnegie and Pace taught Johnson that in dealing with customers, he needed to focus on what they wanted rather than what he wanted.

"When I go in to see people — and I sell an occasional ad now — I never say, 'Help me because I'm black' or 'Help me because I'm a minority.' I always talk about what we can do for them," Johnson explained.

"Sir," Johnson will say, "I want to talk to you about how you can improve your bottom line, how I can increase your sales among black consumers."

Johnson says he also keeps valued employees by getting to know them and their interests.

In the 1960s, when white-owned businesses were starting to hire black professionals, he was worried that some of his best staff might be snatched away. Drawing up a list of his 30 most valuable employees, he asked himself, "What can I do to make people so satisfied they'll never leave me?"

"Once I got to know them," he recalled, "I tried to give them those things they really wanted but would never ask for," such as scholarships for their children. Twenty-eight of those employees remain with him to this day. The other two died.

Johnson delegated freely to his staff but kept close tabs.

When he started out, he recalled, he'd assign a task and say, "I'd like for you to get back to me in 30 days on this. I was naive enough to wait 30 days . . . and they hadn't done anything. I would get angry and dismiss them.

"And then I learned the people I was employing in their place very often weren't as good as they were. People have to be reminded. They have to be pushed."

Although Johnson had to overcome severe racial and economic barriers to achieve his success, he said he found "there are some advantages to disadvantages."

Being born poor, he said, "made me run scared. It made me vow never to go back to welfare, never to go back to poverty. It drives me even today. Some days when I don't feel like getting up, all I have to think about is welfare and humiliation, and I get up early and rush to work."

At the age of 84, Johnson named his daughter CEO of Johnson Publishing in April 2002 but stayed on as active chairman. As he told *Black Enterprise* magazine, "Retirement is not in this company's vocabulary. If you are well and able to work, you can stay at the company and that's what I plan to do."

PART 4

Taking Risks With Management Styles

29

Home Depot's Arthur Blank
And Bernie Marcus
They Rose To The Top By Putting
Customers First

Arthur Blank and Bernie Marcus didn't know where to turn. Unexpectedly fired from their jobs running Handy Dan Home Centers in spring 1978, they felt like middle-aged has-beens.

But they looked at the job loss as an opportunity. They both knew the hardware business. Why not use their experience to create something new?

Blank and Marcus met with an investment banker they knew and told him their idea: a humongous hardware store — the equivalent of 2½ football fields — featuring a tremendous selection and low prices.

Do-it-yourselfers no longer would have to run from hardware store to lumberyard to plumbing supply house every time they worked on a home improvement project.

Impressed by Blank and Marcus's enthusiasm, the banker agreed to back them. The two set about making their vision a reality. They researched markets carefully. They spent every waking moment talking to suppliers, real estate agents and potential employees. They put together a mission statement and stuck to it.

The strategy paid off — in two decades their Home Depot chain had grown to almost 800 stores and $30 billion in sales.

Embracing Change

As the co-founders say in their book, *Built from Scratch*, one of the reasons they've stayed on top is because they continue to change. They try to improve something at their stores every day, whether it's a better display or an expanded approach to customer service.

"Never be satisfied with how things are," Marcus said.

"Retailers can't ever stay the same," Blank said. "If you don't change, you're a dead duck. You must wake up every morning and wonder, 'Who will destroy me today if I don't keep my eyes open?'"

Blank and Marcus decided they needed experts to stay ahead of the game. They began hiring sales associates who had real-life experience: carpenters to man the lumber department, plumbers to run the plumbing department. Their experience allows salespeople to advise customers on anything from gardening to woodworking.

That policy on whom to hire may seem costly — not only are employees paid well for their experience, but they also receive stock options and are promoted from within. Blank and Marcus, though, say the cost is worthwhile.

"Associates have a real vested interest in cultivating customers and building lifelong relationships with them," Blank said. "Payroll is not an expense to us. It's an investment."

In fact, employees are so enthusiastic that Blank and Marcus had to limit managers to working no more than 55 hours a week — a total they'd exceeded regularly.

They'd voluntarily pull all-nighters to get the store ready for opening the next day. Blank and Marcus, however, knew that well-rested employees make better employees. They issued a company-wide memo saying just that.

"People need a balanced life," Blank said. "They need to use their time better."

Blank and Marcus wanted to make sure that the stores and the customers — not the hierarchy at headquarters — remain the focus of the company. Everyone who works for Home Depot starts in the stores — including the corporate counsel.

At first the lawyer balked, but Marcus told him, "If you're going to be handling lawsuits, you're going to have to understand the problems in the store." The attorney conceded and now knows firsthand what employees face daily.

The co-founders treat vendors as partners rather than outside salespeople. They encourage vendors to come into stores, tie on orange Home Depot aprons and work in their appropriate departments. That fosters good communication — vendors understand customer needs, and store employees understand vendor concerns.

Marcus offered an example of how well the partnership works: "Ron Cooper of Price Pfister (Inc.) . . . put aprons on six of his own people and put them to work in our faucet aisle. Then he borrowed two of our people and sent them over to a factory, where they took a tour and offered input on new designs."

The president of another supplier walked into a Home Depot store, stepped up on a ladder and started pulling cartons down from a top shelf.

A sales associate explained that customers weren't allowed on ladders. The man said: "I am only a customer part of the time. I am the president of Dynamic Design, and this stuff needs to be out. I want to pack it down."

So the pair spent the next hour unpacking pots, and Dynamic Design went on to win Vendor of the Year in its category. "These are the kinds of vendors we want," Marcus said.

Blank and Marcus try to learn from every experience. They point to their "don't let the door hit you" experience at Handy Dan and say it taught them to be careful of the kind of people they work with.

It's a practice they apply daily. They scrutinize employees carefully and constantly check each other.

They're even extra-careful of partnerships. Take their start-up experience: Initially, Blank and Marcus reached an agreement with Ross Perot that he would finance the company for $2 million in exchange for 70% ownership.

During the negotiations, Marcus asked if he could keep his 4-year-old Cadillac.

"My people don't drive Cadillacs," Perot said over and over. That's when Blank and Marcus pulled out.

"I knew it wasn't going to work," Marcus said. "If this guy is going to be bothered by what kind of car I'm driving, how much aggravation are we going to have when we have to make a really big decision?"

Perot was the big loser. That $2 million investment was worth $58 billion in 1999.

Financing can be difficult in a start-up. Blank offered one rule of thumb: Whatever you think you're going to need, double it.

"I always tell people starting new companies to secure twice the capital they think they're going to need. Not because [you] need the money, but because it gives [you] the confidence and strength to do what you think is right instead of being pushed by external forces."

No matter how successful your business becomes, monitor it carefully and remember not to take anything for granted, the Home Depot founders say. Blank and Marcus forgot that and bit off more than they could chew.

Checks And Balances

Flush with their own success, Blank and Marcus purchased a competing hardware chain they hadn't thoroughly researched. They soon learned they couldn't handle it — it was too big for their resources, and they had to sell it.

To make sure they didn't repeat the mistake, they persuaded their board of directors to cap annual growth in number of stores at 25% a year. "We wanted the board to protect us from ourselves, and it has," Blank said.

Blank and Marcus say they've prospered because they put customers first. Marcus points to a regional chain he worked for early in his career. The chain failed. The reason? Employees "focused on their own careers and not on the customers," Marcus said.

He was determined that wouldn't happen at Home Depot. Marcus issued a customer bill of rights that everyone in the company must follow.

Shortly after the chain opened its doors in 1979 with four stores in Atlanta, a golfing buddy of Marcus jokingly predicted Home Depot would soon go out of business. He'd come in intending to purchase a $200 faucet, but the sales associate showed him how to fix the one he had for $1.50, thus losing a potential sale.

"You are not the smartest guy in the world," Marcus told his friend, "but if you ever had something go wrong with your household plumbing again, where would you go?"

30

Juniper's Scott Kriens

Willingness To Learn Helped Him Build A Top Networker

I t's not always easy for a top executive to set his employees free to do things on their own.

But at Sunnyvale, Calif.–based Juniper Networks Inc., Chief Executive Scott Kriens has made that freedom the cornerstone on which the company is built.

"We hire the best people in the business, and then we just let them do whatever they want," the then-43-year-old Kriens said in 2000. "Giving them that freedom and responsibility, they will understand the problem and personally own it."

Sticking with that philosophy has helped Kriens build Juniper into an Internet networking powerhouse. Since joining Juniper as CEO in its start-up stages in 1996 to assist in bringing its Internet router to market, Kriens helped it garner more than 10% of the burgeoning $1.4 billion Internet infrastructure market by the end of 2000. That helped him win the 2000 National Ernst & Young Entrepreneur of the Year award.

Kriens credits the people who work for him at Juniper for much of that success. Hiring top-notch workers was a lesson he picked up early in his career, when he worked at networking company Strata-Com Inc., which he helped found. Dick Moley, the chief executive of StrataCom, taught both Kriens and Bill Stensrud, another founder of StrataCom, how vital staffing is.

Upon Stensrud's exit from StrataCom to take over another firm, Moley had one piece of advice for him.

"[Moley] said, 'Hire good people. If you do, nothing else will matter, and if you don't, nothing else will matter,'" Stensrud recalled. "Scott learned that lesson well."

Juniper hires great people who are respected by their peers. That's not novel, but new hires' first job is.

"Their first assignment is to bring in one other person," Kriens said. "The best people attract other like people, because they enjoy their environment. It very much breeds success. It also breeds great loyalty," he said.

The results have been tangible. By the end of 2000, Kriens said Juniper shipped five different platforms and seven different software systems since shipping its first product two years before.

"We have several times the production [of rivals] with fewer people," Kriens said.

Kriens listens to his employees, too. He's instilled in Juniper a philosophy called "Survival of the Fittest Ideas."

"It doesn't matter the office from which an idea came; it purely matters what the quality of the idea is," Kriens said. "That's taking advantage of the quality of the pool of talent you have."

Juniper's nine-member management team sets goals and then moves to the bottom of the organizational chart, Kriens says. Those charged with carrying out those goals then move to the top of the chart, where they're responsible for finding a way to achieve the aims.

Kriens learned many of those principles as his career progressed. He made the switch from computers to networking in 1985. He'd worked in sales at Burroughs Corp. just after he graduated from college in 1979. A few years later, he joined Tandem Computers Inc. in product management. He shifted to the networking business late in his tenure there. Kriens stayed on the networking side when he helped found StrataCom in 1986.

At StrataCom, he says, he was with a team of great people. It just took a while to prove their greatness. The company struggled for five years. Then it changed its market focus and turned a corner.

"The management team was the same," Kriens said. "The first five years, we weren't so smart. The second five, we were geniuses."

That taught him the power of the market and the importance of creating a product or service that's in great demand.

"The market can't be underestimated for its power to create opportunity," Kriens said. "It's important that the markets one chooses are strong and growing."

Kriens left StrataCom in February 1996 to stay home with his wife, who was about to give birth to their first child.

Stensrud had been approached about possibly becoming Juniper's chief executive. He wasn't interested, but he introduced Juniper to Kriens.

Kriens' strengths fit perfectly with what Juniper was looking for. Sales, marketing and execution were his areas of expertise. Juniper already had the engineering know-how.

Stensrud, now a Juniper board member and venture capitalist, says Kriens has always been focused on giving his best.

In their early days together at StrataCom, Stensrud recalls, the company moved its offices into a new location. Kriens, who was one of two regional sales managers, immediately started calling on clients, traveling and working the phones. After five weeks, his office furniture was exactly where the movers had placed it. The other regional sales manager spent four days organizing his office.

Kriens wound up being much more successful at the company.

"Scott has the uncanny ability to home in on things that are important and get people to take action," Stensrud said. He really understands how to spend time on what's important."

Kriens knows the importance of timing. He pushed Juniper to go public when the market was roaring in June 1999.

Investors saw the value. Juniper came public at $6 per share (on a split-adjusted basis). The stock took off and, within a year and a half, traded 25 times higher. Juniper moved into the black in the fourth quarter of 1999.

Kriens, however, remains humble about his role. In fact, he credits the people he's worked with over the years for any pointers he's picked up.

"I've learned more from Dick Moley than from anyone else," Kriens said.

Moley, who became a private investor in the Silicon Valley, recalls a time when StrataCom was forming relationships with original equipment makers in addition to selling directly through its own sales force. Kriens thought it was a mistake to align with Motorola Inc., because it would dwarf StrataCom's sales force. Moley persisted, and the alliance boosted StrataCom's sales. Kriens learned from mistakes like that.

"Today he's an expert at complicated distribution agreements," Moley said.

That learning process didn't stop once Kriens made his mark at Juniper.

"On a really regular basis, he's actively looking for advice," Stensrud said. "He doesn't think he knows it all." Stensrud noted that he sits on many company boards but spends more time giving counsel to successful Juniper than many companies that are struggling.

Kriens knows that the person in charge must occasionally make an unpleasant decision. When he has to make such a move, he makes sure he's done his research and dives in.

"He makes very hard decisions very quickly, and he acts on them," Stensrud said. "Scott is one of a few people who can reach an instinctive decision and act on it quickly."

That helps him avoid a common error.

"The biggest mistake I see leaders make is they probably know something needs to be done, but there's a long lag time before they do it," Stensrud said.

Kriens has just one activity outside work: his family. He has a young daughter and son. They're so important to him that he's instilled a practice at Juniper involving quality time. But Kriens turns that idea upside down.

"My children don't know what quality time is," he said. "They only know how much time I'm there. So at Juniper we spend quality time being intensely focused at work, with people who understand quality time." The result? Kriens typically drops his son off at school at 8 a.m. And he makes sure he's back home from work in time to read him a bedtime story.

31

Executive Ann Fudge

Relies On Lessons Of Youth To Keep Business Growing

A nn Fudge wants to see the same motivating atmosphere at work that she did in her neighborhood when she was growing up.

In her middle-class district in Washington, D.C., "People watched out for everybody," she said. Neighbors kept each other updated about events. People worked together to improve the area. It was the urban equivalent of a home on the range: Seldom was heard a discouraging word.

At her all-girls private school, alumnae — lawyers, government workers — returned regularly to tell the young women that the world was theirs for the taking.

She took them at their word — though at the time the world of business seemed an unlikely destination for a young black woman. Born in 1950, Fudge rose to executive vice president of Kraft Foods Inc. in 1991 and president of its Maxwell House Coffee (1994) and Post Cereals (1997) divisions.

Kraft Foods, the nation's largest food company, is a unit of Philip Morris Cos.

Though her office was in Rye Brook, N.Y., Fudge never forgot the old neighborhood — and how her nurturing there allowed her to strive for success. She applied those lessons every day with her employees.

"One of the most important things someone gets from that kind of background is strong character, personal integrity and courage," she said. "It helps develop you as an individual."

It also helps develop a team. When Fudge hired people, she looked for the same dedication and motivation she saw in her neighborhood role models.

"We hire some very smart people from the very best business schools here," she said. "Beyond the technical ability they bring to the job, what's important is what they bring as a person. We stress the importance of teamwork, of working with people."

Learned From The Negative

Fudge also drew from negative experiences in her youth to stay aware of her employees' needs.

As a black child, she experienced racism. She heard nasty remarks. She saw the blatant exclusion at a large Washington, D.C., department store where black people weren't welcome. She never wants to see it again.

"Anytime you exclude people, you're taking out the full advantage of what [they] have to offer," she said.

So she worked hard to keep all her employees involved. She delegated. She asked for input. She punched up the teamwork message by telling workers that they need to work together tightly to stay ahead of the competition.

That's a lesson she learned by watching the civil rights struggle. People working together toward a common cause can bring great positive change, she saw.

Although teamwork is at the center of her management philosophy, she urges workers to think for themselves and stand up for their ideas. It's ideas — and the people who back them — that help organizations thrive.

"Ideas grow businesses," she said. "You have to be able to come up with an idea, but you also have to be able to champion an idea — sell it."

In late 1994, shortly after she was named president of Maxwell House, Fudge had an innovative idea. Conventional wisdom of the time held that price alone sold coffee and that to increase volume, a company needed to offer coupons or make trade deals with supermarkets to lower prices. Instead, she aimed at creating brand and quality awareness through consumer advertising.

"I really felt it was the right thing to do. A lot of people questioned whether it was," Fudge said.

She refused to listen to naysayers and forged ahead. Her approach paid off.

Although Fudge wouldn't disclose exact figures because of the competitive nature of the coffee and cereal business, she did say the change in marketing approach enabled Maxwell House to "grow our volume and share, and we've more than doubled earnings since then."

If the new approach hadn't worked, she would've tried another, she said. Fudge doesn't dwell on the past. The corporate environment today is too fast-paced. "If [an idea] doesn't work, move on to the next one," she said.

She constantly challenged her staff to be creative. Her mining for ideas went beyond the frequently narrow confines of corporate-think. At meetings she'd throw unusual concepts onto the conference table to see where they led.

Once, after the eBay online auction site announced its purchase of the venerable art auction company Butterfield & Butterfield, she began a meeting by asking staff members to come up with a hypothetical marketing plan for a Kraft brand that would be sold exclusively on the World Wide Web.

That will never happen — but that wasn't the point of the exercise. By keeping people thinking creatively, their ideas will be fresher, she said.

"I continue to drive for innovation to think of different cereal products, take a different approach," she said.

That's how the company came up with concepts for products that have an intentionally limited life span — Maxwell House Holiday Roast, for example. It's how she helped Maxwell House create its own market — the products only appear for a brief time, so people know if they want them, they have to move fast.

Let It Flow

Her employees were eager to keep the ideas coming. Why? Because Fudge let them know she was always open to their suggestions.

"Even though an idea may not work, they won't get beat up," she said. Instead of criticizing workers, "We're going to say, 'Here's what we learned, and we're going to carry over to the next initiative we try.' "

Fudge refused to play either her race or gender card to get ahead. Instead, she always focused entirely on her work.

"I've been black all my life," she said. "I never thought about it. I never think about it. I stay focused on my job. I'm sure people notice when I walk into a room, but I don't want that to define me. I want my capabilities and accomplishments to define me."

Like many women, Fudge needed to make a number of home versus profession choices over the course of her career. She works hard to maintain a balance. "You have to understand the balance between career and family needs," she said.

In that vein, Fudge said she "made decisions that did not move her career forward in a rapid manner." But she said devoting time to her family and striving for a balance between work and home made her a better executive and finds the proof in her success.

The wife, mother of two and grandmother of two said she understands that balance means happier employees. Happier employees make better workers, she said.

Fudge noted that she also has a responsibility to her grandchildren — and the grandchildren of the world. "Our young people should really believe in their dreams and know they can do it. As adults we have to keep the spirit of hope and optimism alive in our young people."

Fudge, having left Kraft in late 2001, was named chairwoman and chief executive of Young & Rubicam Advertising in May 2003.

32

Coca-Cola's Robert Woodruff
He Made The Real Thing

Robert Woodruff was no slacker when it came to quality. And to get it from his employees, he sometimes stirred things up.

One day in 1926, the chief executive of Coca-Cola Co. called his salesmen together. He said their jobs would no longer exist, so they were fired. Woodruff added, however, that the firm planned to create a brand-new position. Those interested could attend a meeting the next day.

The nervous men showed up, and Woodruff pitched his new plan. He wanted all of them in the room to toss their "salesman" titles and take on the new role of "serviceman." Getting Coca-Cola to the soda fountains across the nation wasn't enough, Woodruff thought. In order to win, the firm had to become No. 1 in service. Each serviceman was assigned to a new territory.

Coca-Cola's service staff strove for what Woodruff wanted: ensuring that the soda fountains served each glass of the soft drink at its best.

Woodruff (1889–1985) became Coca-Cola's CEO in April 1923 and held the position for 31 years. By the time he retired in 1954, the former pharmacy-born elixir had grown into a global beverage with $7 billion in sales. Coca-Cola remains one of America's best-known consumer brands.

How did a man with poor grades in school and no background in the beverage industry score so much success?

The former truck salesman figured he had a winning product in Coca-Cola. So instead of trying to make drastic changes, he focused on ways to keep customers and to make the drink better.

Setting Standards

To keep quality even, Woodruff standardized everything regarding the drink.

He set up a fountain training school to teach servicemen and vendors the proper way to serve Coca-Cola. Students learned that the ideal temperature at which to serve the drink was 34 degrees Fahrenheit. Instructors taught the servicemen to remember, "It's gotta be cold if it's gonna be sold."

To enhance the drink's taste, they instructed fountain servers to serve it only in a specially designed bell-shaped glass. Servers also had to use shaved ice made with special six-pronged ice forks supplied by Coca-Cola.

Woodruff also stressed a high level of hygiene at every plant.

One day in 1924, he stepped into a plant and found a carpet of dust on the machines, broken bottles in one corner, and flies sucking up spilled syrup everywhere, Mark Pendergrast wrote in *For God, Country and Coca-Cola*. Woodruff demanded that the factory owner shape up or ship out. The owner replied it wouldn't do any good because the next day it would look the same again. So Woodruff slowly took his cigar out of his mouth, looked straight at the man and said, "You wipe your [behind], don't you?"

Standardization wasn't limited to production. Bookkeeping practices, the color of trucks, even the driver uniforms all had to be the same. In any form of advertising, the name "Coca-Cola" couldn't be broken up into two lines, no matter how small the ad, Howard Means wrote in *Money & Power: The History of Business*.

Wouldn't Go Negative

In the 1920s, negative ads were status quo in the industry. Big companies tried to feed on consumers' fears. Hoover Vacuum ads proclaimed that "Dirty Rugs Are Dangerous," Pendergrast wrote. Scott Tissues, Gillette and other big companies also tried to scare the consumer into using their wares.

Woodruff refused to go along. His policy was no negative ads. Why? He wanted people to drink Coca-Cola as a means to enjoy a relaxing moment during their busy lives.

It wasn't just a drink, he contended, but a way of life.

So he spent time and resources on creating a positive, feel-good brand. With help from the D'Arcy ad agency, Woodruff soon found the words he wanted to describe Coke. Billboards stretched across rural and urban America carrying phrases such as "The Pause That Refreshes," "Bounce Back to Normal," and "Always Delightful."

Woodruff also backed the hiring of top painters to create images that associated Coke with the best that the American way of life had to offer. Norman Rockwell's painting of a freckled boy sitting with his dog, fishing pole and a Coca-Cola bottle was one of many ads that perfected the drink's image.

In the U.S. and Europe, Santa Claus was depicted as tall and gaunt or as an elf, dressed in blue, yellow or other colors. In 1931, Coca-Cola ran ads painted by Haddon Sundblom of Santa as a jolly fat man with a Coke bottle in hand, donning black boots, a wide belt and dressed in Coca-Cola red. That rendition of Santa has stuck ever since.

Woodruff knew mass advertising alone couldn't drive sales. So he strove to make Coca-Cola available in as many places as possible.

Growing With America

As more and more people traveled, gas stations spread across the country. Woodruff spotted this trend. So the firm developed and sold coolers, vending machines, dispensing equipment and displays to make Coca-Cola "within an arm's reach of desire."

Woodruff believed in intensive market research to keep growing.

In the late 1920s, Coca-Cola had bottling plants in nearly every town and made it into all of the 115,000 soda fountains across the U.S. So Woodruff asked the statistics department to find out if Coca-Cola had reached a saturation point.

After a three-year study of 15,000 retail outlets, they found a close tie between traffic flow and sales volume. Woodruff learned that dealers with the highest sales tended to have the largest number of passers-by as potential new customers. But these outlets had few Coca-Cola signs inside or outside the store.

Armed with this knowledge, Woodruff deployed servicemen to visit these hot spots more often and offer special services. Then the marketing research team got into full swing again, surveying 42,000 drugstore customers, Pendergrast wrote. They found that 22% of those who tried Coke made a second purchase at some other counter.

33

Entrepreneur Michael Dell

How He Made His Firm The
Fastest-Growing Computer Maker

When Michael Dell promotes employees, he gives them fewer responsibilities, not more.

That may sound wacky, but the strategy — which Dell calls "job segmentation" — has been key to ensuring his company's growth hasn't led to flameout.

From 1994 to 1999, earnings at Dell Computer Corp. surged by an annual average of 91%. Sales in the same period grew by an annual average of 48%.

Within 15 years of starting his made-to-order-computer business in 1984, Michael Dell turned Dell Computer into an $18 billion international company. In the first quarter of 2001, Dell Computer became the world's No. 1 PC maker, surpassing Compaq for the top spot.

"When a business is growing quickly, many jobs grow laterally in responsibility, becoming too big and complex for even the most ambitious, hardest-working person to handle without sacrificing personal career development or becoming burned out," Dell wrote in his 1999 book, *Direct from Dell: Strategies That Revolutionized an Industry.*

When Dell started job segmentation in the mid-1990s, employees were confused. But the company's explosive growth as the leading direct marketer of computers revealed the necessity of the plan. Even when managers' business units were divided in half, those managers were soon overseeing entities that were bigger than their original units.

Trying It On

Dell's also applied the strategy to himself.

Feeling overwhelmed, he brought in Mort Topfer, a Motorola Inc. executive, in 1994 to share the office of the chairman. Dell focused on products, technology and overall strategy. Topfer, who retired in December 2001, handled operations, sales and marketing.

While Dell was working with customers on product development and quality control, giving speeches and meeting with the press, Topfer focused on the day-to-day duties.

In 1997, Dell segmented his job again, pulling Kevin Rollins, who headed company operations for the Americas, up the ranks. Rollins served as a vice chairman for four years and took on the responsibilities of president and chief operating officer in March 2001. He and Dell work together to set the company's strategic direction.

"I believe pretty strongly that you shouldn't limit a company by one person's ego or by the abilities of any one person," he said.

"I've been very aggressive in sharing responsibilities with others. And it's actually been quite easy, because there's much too much to be done. I'm much more focused on getting it done than who did it or who got the credit," he said in a 1999 interview.

That spirit is behind another key strategy at the Round Rock, Texas, corporation: "Everyone's job includes finding and developing their successor — not just when they are ready to move into a new role, but as an ongoing part of their performance plan," Dell wrote.

Thanks to the company's rapid growth, few workers have stayed in the same jobs for long. Dell, who started the company in his University of Texas dorm room with $1,000 in capital in 1983, built it into a global titan that boasted more than 39,000 employees in 2003.

He learned one lesson early: Don't hire someone based on the company's immediate job needs. Hire a candidate based on his or her potential to grow and develop.

Success requires one "to add talent and organize a business correctly," Dell said.

He describes the ideal Dell employee as having an open and questioning mind, a healthy balance of experience and intellect and an eagerness to innovate even though the process will entail mistakes.

As the company has expanded, the chief executive has made a point of staying involved in the details. That allows him and other top brass to make quick decisions, he says, because they already know the specific issues at hand.

How does he stay in the thick of things? Roaming around, both physically and in cyberspace, he gets candid comments from employees and customers. It's more important to know your customers than to know your competitors, Dell says.

His best customers aren't the ones who buy the most or require the least help, he says. They're the ones who teach the company the most.

The company learns through more than 300,000 telephone, online and face-to-face interactions each week. Dell himself doesn't keep his distance. He spends 40% of his time with the people who pay him. He'll anonymously log on to chat rooms where ordinary users talk about the company and its competitors, and he sometimes monitors customer-service phone calls.

"I want to come upon someone who's teaching an elderly woman how to turn her system on for the first time," he wrote. "I want to happen upon someone who is stumped by a customer's question — and help answer it if I can."

When asked why he devotes so much of his time to customers, he replied, "I thought that was my job."

Brown-Bagging It

To get unrehearsed feedback from employees, he shows up unannounced at the factory and attends brown-bag lunches with people from all over the company.

Dell says his company is allergic to hierarchy. If he has a problem, he won't handle it through middle management. He'll go to the person who's directly responsible. At the same time, employees are encouraged to ask him questions, either at meetings or via e-mail.

Staying on the cutting edge makes it necessary for employees to embrace new technology, Dell says. That's required some creative approaches at his corporation. For instance, Dell realized in the mid-1990s that the Internet would be key to his business. But he had to get his employees behind the idea.

Dell developed an online literacy quiz called "Know the Net" and asked his employees to take it. He staged a scavenger hunt, getting people to find information on the Web.

Some questioned whether employees might use the Net to slack off. But Dell thought that was ludicrous. "That's like saying, 'We don't want to teach our people how to read because they might spend all their time reading,'" he wrote.

Dell faced similar challenges in the mid-1980s when he had to persuade employees to use electronic mail. His technique then was simply to ask them whether they'd gotten the note he'd sent via e-mail.

"No one likes to be uninformed, right?" he wrote.

Immersing his employees in the Net early on appears to have paid off. A year after starting to sell products over the Internet in 1996, Dell was the first company to record online sales of $1 million. Dell's Web site, www.dell.com, ultimately became one of the highest-volume commerce sites on Windows-based operating systems in the world.

34

Nokia's Jorma Ollila

With Innovation And Insight, He Made His Company No. 1

Chief Executive Jorma Ollila of Nokia Corp. called his four division managers to the conference room of the firm's glass Helsinki headquarters building and made a startling request.

Would they please swap jobs with each other?

It was a puzzling directive, given that this was the group that was powering Nokia's successful sprint past longtime leader Motorola Inc. in 1998 to become No. 1 in the sexiest field in telecommunications — making wireless phones.

In 1999, Nokia snapped up 27% of the global market for cellular handsets. Motorola was in second place with a 17% share, according to Bryan Prohm, a mobile-communications analyst with market researcher Dataquest Inc. Why mess with an arrangement that was working so well?

Because Finnish leader Ollila's "everyone-out-of-your-comfort-zone" management style is a proven winner. He pushed the firm — invisible in the 1980s — to dominance in the 1990s. The managerial musical chairs was another instance of the CEO's approach to keeping a company fresh and innovative.

"I want to remove stubbornness that gets built into the minds of people," Ollila told *BusinessWeek* in 1998. "We want to build a certain amount of chaos and a sense of urgency. Switching also helps people learn from one another. . . . It's cross-fertilization."

Nokia's annual earnings show Ollila's approach is on target. The firm doubled revenue from $10 billion in 1997 to $20.6 billion in

1999. Earnings soared from 96 cents per share in 1997 to $2.26 in 1999. Even through the sluggish economic start of the 21st century, Nokia has managed to increase or maintain its revenue.

After 1999 earnings were reported, the company's stock price rocketed to more than $200 a share — more than doubling since October of that year — giving the firm a $247 billion value.

"The whole story of Nokia is kind of like *Alice in Wonderland*," said Ray Jodoin, a senior global wireless analyst with Cahners In-Stat Group. That such powerful leadership comes from such a laid-back Finn, who loves his sauna hot and his tennis game hotter, might seem strange. But that's typical of the surprises provided by Nokia, a company many have mistakenly believed was a Japanese or Korean concern.

More than 135 years after the company was founded as a paper manufacturer, Nokia's CEO (born Aug. 15, 1950) spends his days at the cutting edge of high tech, working to place the Internet, he said, "into everyone's pocket."

Ollila gives the credit for Nokia's lead to the firm's more than 50,000 employees. Ollila has put a great deal of effort into designing a corporate system that allows each employee to give 110%.

Frank Nuovo, Nokia's chief mobile-phone designer, credits that system for creating an extraordinary sense of teamwork and a hothouse of innovation.

Ollila knew that communication between marketing people and designers feeds the creative process, and he looked for ways to inspire innovation, Nuovo says.

"Meetings in different places — like outdoors by a lake — are good for the creative process. We work like a jazz band. We work off of each other," Nuovo said.

One reason Nokia's products are so successful is that Ollila's made sure the firm's many departments are connected. For instance, he brought Nokia's research-and-development operations — which in 2000 included 36 centers, 8,000 employees and a $1 billion annual budget — into direct touch with customers.

As Ollila suspected, once R&D workers heard firsthand what customers wanted, things changed. The company hired trendy California designers, and phones became colorful and flashy.

"They really seem to take the time to find out what the customer wants," analyst Jodoin said.

Knowing that growth comes from boldness and that mistakes can teach valuable lessons, Ollila's standing policy is not to fire anyone. After company share prices fell by half in 1995, Ollila refused to listen to cries for managers' heads. Instead, he realigned departments, interviewing managers and figuring out who had the newest ideas for the different areas. Quickly, he fixed the blips and got the company back on track.

Ollila's stellar turnaround of Nokia — in 1990 a money-losing conglomerate — brings admiration from executives and loyalty from employees.

Ollila, who joined Nokia in 1985 as vice president of international operations and became senior vice president of finance in 1986, has never been afraid to try something unusual. When he managed the company's mobile-phone division from 1990 to 1992, he experimented with design. He pored over the competition's offerings. He made sure Nokia's prices were better. Sales soared. The company board liked his style and gave Ollila the CEO post in 1992.

Aware that he was good at what he knew, he began transforming the company into a mobile-phone powerhouse. To expand Nokia, he figured, the company needed more outlets. So he snapped up Europe's cell phone retail market piece by piece. It was a move that proved key to the firm's dominant position today.

"[Ollila] stepped on the gas pedal at Nokia, pushing what mobile phones could do: better battery performance; getting away from black and gray into chrome and colors," said Prohm, the Dataquest analyst.

The result was a quadrupling of sales of handsets for consumers and cell base-station stations for service providers, from $2.1 billion in 1993 to $8.7 billion in 1997. By 2000, 90% of Nokia's revenue came from cell phones, base stations and base-station software. The company also produces multimedia terminals and computer monitors.

Ollila's long focused on his vision of a wireless world in which a customer's cell phone connects him to the Internet and everyone else. It looks as if it's fast becoming reality. In 2000, cell phones numbered about 500 million worldwide, according to Jodoin. By the end of 2002, more than 1 billion cell phones were ringing. That means a doubling of the market in less than three years.

To keep the market moving forward, Ollila's pushing the third generation of information technology at Nokia. The first generation was analog, the second digital. The third generation is a technological leap that will move massive amounts of information quickly through the Internet and onto a customer's cell phone.

Think banking while walking down the street, scanning apartment rental ads from a car or watching a videoconference while tanning on the beach.

Preparing and protecting Nokia's place in that future keeps Ollila busy. Competition is getting stronger.

Japan's Sony Corp. has formed a joint venture with Nokia competitor, Stockholm, Sweden–based L.M. Ericsson Telephone Co., to produce multimedia cell phones. Ericsson has also teamed up with Microsoft Corp. to create Web-browsing software for its phones. Third-place Ericsson held about 12% of 1999's global cell phone market.

Second-place Motorola, whose market share is about half that of Nokia in 2003, has finally corrected course from analog and is back in the game with a new generation of digital handsets. Other matters of concern for Ollila include handset prices that are sure eventually to follow calculator prices and plummet.

But Nokia's board members aren't worried. Ollila remains confident that his drive to do what it takes to finish first will keep the concern sailing along.

Should directors grow nervous, they need only walk outside headquarters and stroll the streets of Helsinki. There, they will witness Finnish teen-agers flashing short text messages back and forth on their red and blue Nokia phones. Three of every four Finnish cell phones are Nokias.

35

Harley-Davidson's Jeffrey Bleustein

Communication Focus Keeps His Company Roaring

Jeffrey Bleustein was revved up. It was mid-November, and the chairman and chief executive of motorcycle king Harley-Davidson Inc. was fresh from a six-hour town hall meeting at a company factory. There, Bleustein held court with roughly 800 employees in separate sessions for each of the three shifts.

In the first five minutes, he brought each group up to speed on the motorcycle market, Harley's performance and market share data. Then he opened the floor to questions.

Bleustein believes in free exchange of communication with his stakeholders — who range from customers, employees and investors to suppliers. He insists on face-to-face meetings so he can read emotions and feelings. This way, he gets to know their needs and they his so they develop a mutually productive, trusting relationship.

He also gleans ideas this way. At this meeting, one employee thought it would help assembly-line workers do their jobs better if they could take the same course on servicing motorcycles that was offered to Harley dealers.

Bleustein didn't think it would work to enroll hundreds more into the already crowded two-week training program. But he's mulling over a special, 12-hour version of the course for assembly-line workers that would be given on the factory floors.

Bleustein holds a town hall meeting once a year at each company site so he's sure to meet all 7,000 Harley employees. In addition, general managers at each locale meet with employees monthly. He also looks for opportunities to talk with employees daily.

In fact, Bleustein tries to make himself available to all his constituencies.

"There's no way to do that by sitting in the office and guessing," he said in an interview. "You need to spend time together, to develop relationships so that you really get at the heart of what's important in the relationship."

To get firsthand market research, Bleustein and his wife, Brenda, go to 6 to 12 Harley Owners Group (HOG) rallies a year, most of which draw crowds of 100,000 to 300,000 Harley-Davidson aficionados. Bleustein and other executives mingle and ride with customers and encourage them to discuss what's on their minds, problems and even dreams. He and other managers use the ideas they get from these rallies to develop new models and programs. That's how Harley came up with the training program dealers give customers who are new to the sport.

After a six-year stint teaching engineering and applied science at Yale University, Bleustein joined Harley in 1975 as vice president of engineering. He spent the next nine years making major contributions to revitalizing and expanding its product line.

Looking for a way to challenge himself and build a sparkling new image for the company, Bleustein in 1981 became one of 13 managers who bought near-bankrupt Harley from AMF Inc. In 1997, after holding various senior executive spots, he became president and CEO of Harley-Davidson Inc. at age 57. He added chairman to his title in 1998 and relinquished the presidency in 2001.

Harley, based in Milwaukee, is No. 1 in the U.S. market in heavyweight motorcycles. Thanks to better-quality products over the years and new programs, many of which were spawned under Bleustein, demand for its bikes far outstrip supply. Besides the bikes, Harley sells everything from bike parts and accessories to riding clothes and accessories.

In 2000, Harley posted its 15th straight year of record results. In 1999 and 2000, earnings surged at a 26% average annual rate and sales at a 19% rate. From the end of 1998 to early 2001, its stock more than doubled. 2002 was Harley's 17th consecutive year of record revenue and net income.

Key to the company's success is its leadership style, built around the notion of management by group consensus. This concept has evolved over the years and was put in place in 1993, when Bleustein was president and chief operating officer of the Harley-Davidson Motor Co. unit.

The company is organized into three circles: sales and marketing; manufacturing, engineering and purchasing in operations; and finance and human resources.

A group, made up of Bleustein and elected members of the three circles, is the leadership and strategy council. This group oversees the issues that go across all circles and apply to the whole company. They deal with decisions that can't be left to individual groups, says Bleustein, such as allocating resources and creating budgets.

Bleustein urges each person in the company to take a role in decision making, rather than waiting for direction from the top. To get employees to participate in the change process, Bleustein helps them paint a picture of the new state of affairs and creates a vision of where they're headed.

"I try to help the group define what they want to be in the future and then [how to] get there," said Bleustein. "If it's a compelling enough vision, people will work for it, even if it's hard to get there."

For instance, in the early 1990s, Harley was struggling to get the bottlenecks out of the manufacturing process because it hadn't done enough long-range planning. Management solved the problem, in part, by changing the process. But Bleustein and other executives wanted to avert problems down the road.

So in 1993 Bleustein called on union members and employees to help craft a long-range plan. The goal was aggressive: By its 100th anniversary in 2003, it would be able to build and sell 200,000 bikes compared with the 80,000 bikes a year it was making at the time. There were lots of skeptics.

"But then we painted a picture and said, 'OK, if we were there, this is what it would look like.' Everyone liked the picture and decided to go for it. As it turned out, we're going to achieve the goal [of making 200,000 bikes] two years in advance," he said in 2001.

"Because we involved a great many people to put together the plan, they were committed to making it work and making tremendous changes in the way we worked together to make it come true." Harley-Davidson's revised 2003 production goal? A mere 289,000 bikes.

Before they even celebrated that 100th anniversary, Bleustein and his team started mapping out the next 10 years.

Bleustein's engineering background has helped him feel comfortable with figures and doing analysis. But it hasn't been key to his success as a leader.

"The most important thing about leadership is getting tied to people, figuring out how to bring the best out of people and how to create the environment where people can rise to their full potential," he said.

Keeping that in mind, Bleustein tries to ensure that everyone in the company has access to the same information.

"If you don't give them the information they need, they see only half the picture, won't be able to make the decision and will opt out," he said. "But if you give people the same information, we find people throughout the company tend to make the same decisions."

To achieve that, Harley distributes plenty of booklets, memos and e-mails mapping out goals, behavior standards and corporate values.

Bleustein also makes sure Harley communicates its goals and achievements with consumers — and keeps them happy.

"We concentrate not just on product, but on the entire experience to make sure customers get great, quality products and have opportunities and reasons to use those products," he said.

When asked what the experience of driving a Harley was like, he said: "One of our T-shirts says, 'If I have to explain it, you won't understand.'"

36

Sesame Street's
Joan Ganz Cooney
The ABCs Of Creating A Classic

To reach the top of her field, Joan Ganz Cooney has relied on the cream of the crop.

To make a concept in any field work, "you [can't] be afraid of very, very talented people around you," Cooney said in an interview. "You've got to go for the best; you've got to go for people who can replace you if something happened to you."

Cooney is the originator of *Sesame Street* and the driving force behind it. The highly acclaimed preschool show, which has won 86 Emmy Awards (the most of any TV show ever) for its unique blend of education and entertainment, began its 34th season in April 2003. It's been seen in more than 140 countries.

"I would not have been able to do what we did here without having an immensely talented group of allies and aides within the company who had various talents I didn't have," she said. "The stronger and talented a person was, the happier I was."

In 1968, Cooney co-founded the nonprofit Children's Television Workshop (called Sesame Workshop since 2000), the company that produces *Sesame Street*. It also produces *Dragon Tales* and *Sagwa the Chinese-Siamese Cat*. Cooney served as CTW's chief executive from 1968 to 1990.

She received the Presidential Medal of Freedom in 1995, the nation's highest civilian honor, for her work. Currently, Cooney is Sesame Workshop's chairman of the executive committee and vice chairman of the board. Her two successors as chief executive were promoted from within.

"She hires very smart people who are very dedicated and committed to the workshop and its mission," said Jeff Watanabe, the current chairman of Sesame Workshop.

Cooney gives her employees broad autonomy to do their jobs, as well as a voice in how she's doing hers. "I liked being argued with. I liked being told I was wrong," Cooney said. "By and large I was saved from many, many errors and wrong turns by people who argued with me and made their case. Anyone who challenges the CEO really should be listened to, because they're not going to do it lightly."

To build a team atmosphere, Cooney says "we" rather than "I" when talking with co-workers.

"Joan has a personal warmth and respect for the people she was dealing with that came across, so that even though she was making decisions that might displease them, they still felt that she appreciated them personally," said Lloyd Morrisett, co-founder of CTW and chairman emeritus of the Sesame Workshop's board of trustees.

Cooney has long soaked up the advice of others. She says that one of the best suggestions she received when she was starting out with *Sesame Street* was from Fred Friendly, then head of CBS News. He was also a consultant to the Ford Foundation, one of *Sesame Street's* original funders.

"[Friendly] said to me to be careful that you never allow a 'consensus of negatives' to build," Cooney recalled. "I never forgot that phrase. Don't let one or two negatives pile up and say that it doesn't mean anything. [For example,] criticism starts that your people are not very nice to deal with, and then [someone says] that you're going for the wrong airtime or being too heavy-handed in trying to get it. Try to avert negatives in the first place, or when they come up, try to deal with them right away."

Cooney had a definite goal upon graduating from the University of Arizona in 1951.

"I was driven, almost from the time I graduated, by a sense of idealism and wanting to make some difference with my life," she said.

She saw that chance in TV. Cooney became a public affairs producer of documentaries and talk shows in New York City. One of her documentaries covered preschool education.

It was then that Morrisett — a friend of hers and vice president of Carnegie Corp. at the time — asked her if she'd be interested in doing a study to examine the education potential of TV programming for young children. Cooney's subsequent feasibility report and research showed the idea had merit. *Sesame Street* was born out of that.

"From the very beginning she had a vision about what she wanted to accomplish," Morrisett said.

From her research, Cooney narrowed her goals for *Sesame Street* to just two: It had to be entertaining to children and also had to educate them in a concrete, verifiable way.

To ensure that was the case, she had an educational testing service go into preschools. They tested children after they watched the show to see how much the children had learned. In addition, researchers observed children watching the show to see if there were any segments where their attention span waned.

Cooney still believes field research is a necessity, and she's insisted on it throughout the life of the workshop. "You better do it. The TV world changes, and so does what children like on television," she said.

Through all of the achievements of *Sesame Street*, one thing that hasn't changed is Cooney.

"Joan's been somebody who pushes for improvement," said Gary Knell, the current CEO of Sesame Workshop. "Other people would have retired, but she has a keen interest in not just keeping [*Sesame Street*] alive but in keeping it vibrant. Joan's really in many ways kept us true to the brand and the trust that we've built with parents for now almost three generations.

"*Sesame Street's* won more Emmys now than any show in the history of television, 86. That doesn't really mean anything to a 4-year-old child who's got a remote control today. You've got to keep the program vibrant and interesting for that kid. Joan, instead of resting on her laurels, of which there have been many deserved laurels, has really pushed to keep improving, to keep making it better."

Success comes from effort, Cooney maintains. "You have to have some luck in all this, but you also make your own luck and get a focus on what you'd like to do," she said.

"You don't necessarily start [your career] where you're going to finish, but you try to get on the road you want to be on and keep an immense amount of focus. And be prepared to work hard."

37

SEI Investments'
Alfred P. West Jr.

Amid Success, He Rededicated
Company To Coping With Change

Alfred P. West Jr. could easily have been content. In 1990, SEI Investments Co., which he'd founded 22 years earlier, seemed, by all accounts, to be gliding along smoothly. Revenue was growing at a steady 15% to 20% annual rate.

Still, he wasn't satisfied with just doing well. Laid up with a broken leg from a skiing accident, West took the opportunity to step back and examine his company, a provider of technology and asset management services to institutional investors.

He found it was no longer the spry, consumer-focused business he'd started after gaining his MBA from The Wharton School at the University of Pennsylvania in 1966.

"We had had a hardening of the arteries as we were growing up," West said. "I felt we were not adapting well to a changing environment."

West didn't just try to fix things around the edges with pep rallies or a lot of talk. He was determined to reinvigorate SEI, and he didn't believe in half measures. Instead, West undertook a complete restructuring, breaking down barriers that had the company's three divisions competing against each other rather than working together to serve clients.

Results didn't come overnight. But West's moves laid the groundwork for an acceleration in revenue over the coming years. In 2000, SEI's revenue grew 31%, double its rate a decade before.

"Our earnings went up during that [restructuring] period," West said, though not as much as some on Wall Street would have liked. "But we stuck to our guns."

West didn't have the support of his division heads when he set about revamping the company, but he didn't wait for their approval. He pushed ahead with changes because he believed he was right.

"A consensus was impossible, because I had three divisions at the time led by three strong individuals," West said. "They had their fiefdoms and wanted to keep things the way they were, but [I] wanted to create a much more collaborative environment."

West summoned the courage to take a risk. He knew where he wanted to lead and was willing to part with those who didn't like the direction, says Henry Greer, SEI's former president, who stayed on as a board member.

"His leadership was tested during SEI's reinvention," Greer said. "We tore apart the organization and changed the culture of the company. [West] was the one who came up with the concept and really orchestrated the transformation. There were just a few of us who stood out in embracing this new philosophy, but perseverance won out."

SEI lost half its employees over the next three years, including its three division heads.

"Those were the people that did not want change," West said.

West believes being willing to embrace change is a key element in success.

"If you're totally comfortable, then somebody's going to sneak up behind you. If you're not innovating, that means you're going to be left behind," he said.

West wanted to re-create the entrepreneurial spirit SEI enjoyed when it was new and focused on customer service. "We all knew the client [then], and we just gave so much better service, and we were so much better in touch with the business," he said.

West doesn't believe restructuring to be solely an internal matter. He believes in putting clients first. He made sure SEI's clients were apprised of the changes, Greer says.

"We brought clients in to see what our new culture was about, how we were trying to reconstruct the business to provide the best possible service," Greer said. "We made sure they knew they were part of the equation."

West doesn't leave his employees any room for doubt about his priorities. The company moved into a new corporate headquarters in Oaks, Pa., with no walls, rubber floors and furniture that's all on wheels so it can be moved in an instant. Telephone and electric cables come down from the ceiling, enabling employees to hook up quickly at their new locations.

There are no floor plans, no permanent seating chart and no secretaries, so no one gets too comfortable. In fact, the company uses a software program to keep track of everyone's whereabouts in the office.

West wasn't unafraid of being unconventional, even though SEI competes in the buttoned-down banking and asset management world.

"We flattened the management structure and got everything out of the way," West said. "I wanted to create a culture of 'Let's try it.'"

West devised an environment in which new leaders could come forward. The company is composed of self-managed teams, with new teams forming to take on new challenges.

"We call it fluid leadership," West told *Fast Company* magazine in April 1998. "People figure out what they're good at, and that shapes what their roles are. There's not just one leader. Different people lead during different parts of the process."

Authority isn't just delegated to employees. Instead, it's up to members of a team to assume leadership roles.

"I believe in managing by setting a vision and a strategy," said West. "I'll have an agenda, but it won't be a micromanagement agenda. I'm very much more of a coach and a coordinator."

West reinforces his belief in a team-oriented approach by providing incentives.

"It's not a zero-sum game," West said. "We have a very large incentive plan, and it's based on company performance and unit performance and team performance, and it is a high percentage of an individual's annual compensation."

The teamwork and new corporate culture West fostered had a specific purpose — improving the company's financial performance and delivering for shareholders.

West believes it's important to have a firm goal in mind and a road map for getting there. He also believes in aiming high.

"I'm a big believer that if you don't put out goals that are significant stretches, you don't get outside of your box," West said. "If you put out a goal that is achievable, there's no pressure. There's no stress."

In 1997, he set the goal for SEI to earn $5 a share in 2000, up from $1.40 in 1997.

"People [inside the company] said there is no way," West said. "That was a big goal, and we're on track. We had to really decide what was going to get us there and where we were going to put the resources to get us there."

That process required a full examination of every aspect of the company's business and its prospects, West says.

"We divided our investments and our units into three groups. One group was areas that were doing great that we needed to do more of, keep stoking the fires and giving them investment; another group was businesses that really needed reinventing; and a third group was brand-new things we needed to stoke faster," he said.

SEI had earnings per share of $3.54 in 1999. In 2000, it surpassed West's goal with an EPS of $5.22 (adjusted for a 3:1 and a 2:1 stock split).

Before it even met those earlier earnings goals, SEI already set a new target of tripling earnings per share in three years. Someone doesn't take the pressure off just because he's met his goals, West says.

By making a list of priorities, West keeps his eyes on the ball.

"I'm a big list maker," he said. "That keeps me focused, so I don't just do the easy stuff."

PART 5

Keeping The Customer In Mind

38

eBay's Meg Whitman
Why This Dot-Com Keeps Growing

In 1996, eBay was little more than a glorified flea market selling a relative handful of used items. Two years later, incoming Chief Executive Meg Whitman launched an expansion plan that became the envy of Internet firms worldwide.

The year she took over, annual revenue was $6 million. In 2001, it topped $748 million. Sales for 2002 exceeded $1.2 billion.

Whitman has kept eBay growing amid technical setbacks and a Web minefield of "dot-bomb" explosions.

The company, which sells new and used merchandise in a wide range of categories, had 62 million registered users at the end of 2002.

Growth Strategy

Whitman's tools for growth? Persistence and vision.

She continues defying the odds because she makes sure she knows her market, adapts quickly to change and builds momentum by delivering new user options and an expanding list of product categories.

Whitman's grown the company in large part by quickly spotting customer trends. As soon as a product category sprouts legs, she plays it up, ensuring maximum buzz on user bulletin boards.

Whitman fends off competitors with a simple philosophy: Customers rule. Part of her strategy? Consistently working user input into daily operations.

Several times a year, she flies customers to eBay headquarters to get their take on ideas in development and to seek ways that services can be streamlined. She listens intently, flagging ideas for later use. Weeks later, she follows up with conference calls that include the same customers to fine-tune adjustments.

"Users are the company," Whitman said. "They're the ones who bring the product and merchandise it."

Whitman knows that the more options users have, the more often they'll return. In 2002, she expanded the number of fixed-price products — an alternative for those who'd rather buy without bidding.

Raising The Bar

Part of her secret is setting big goals and mapping proven strategies to reach them.

Her revenue goal for 2005 is $3 billion. She announced the objective in 2000 and remains confident she'll hit it. How? By continuing to attract top management talent and by "building our back-end infrastructure," she said.

In 2002, Whitman bought the transaction service firm PayPal to reduce processing costs. It replaced an unprofitable in-house credit card unit.

On a number of goals, Whitman has hit pay dirt ahead of schedule. She grew profit faster than expected by cutting costs and adding merchandise. To raise eBay's profile, she established local sites in more than 50 U.S. cities.

She also hedged her bets with overseas targets. Net revenue from foreign markets — 27 countries in all — was $109.1 million in the fourth quarter of 2002, up 173% from the same year-ago period.

Japan has been eBay's only foreign glitch. The company entered the market too late, giving Yahoo! a stronger-than-expected head start. Whitman learned from the mistake and pulled out earlier this year.

Correcting mistakes quickly may be her ultimate success secret. Instead of dwelling on errors, she turns on a dime and looks for new challenges.

39

AOL's Steve Case

He Built An Online Empire By
Keeping The Customer In Mind

A s a child growing up in Honolulu, Steve Case sold seeds, watches and Christmas cards to customers on his newspaper route.

"I'm not sure how I got the idea," the then-41-year-old Case said in a 2000 interview, "but I was interested in little businesses and making some money, so the newspaper route was one way to do that. It seemed like a sensible thing to do."

Years later, Case used a similar strategy to make his company, Dulles, Va.–based America Online Inc., the largest Internet service provider in the world.

From its founding in 1985, AOL grew to 21 million subscribers by 2000. By the end of 2002 that number had risen to 35.2 million. Members of this burgeoning online community use AOL to surf the Web, send electronic mail, communicate in chat rooms and purchase products on the Web. In 2001, AOL members in the U.S. spent about $33 billion online.

Case was responsible for AOL's fast growth, which is unmatched in any industry, says Dan Akerson, chairman of Nextel Communications Inc., chief executive of Nextlink Communications Inc. and an AOL board member.

"Steve believed in his vision and built the company according to that vision. He is not afraid to buck conventional wisdom. He is truly a pioneer," Akerson said.

In January 2001, Case put together AOL's $112 billion merger with Time Warner Inc., creating a multimedia conglomerate with

Internet, print, television and movie interests. AOL, whose stock value was double that of Time Warner's prior to the merger, got 55% of the combined company. In early 2003, Case announced he would step down as chairman of AOL Time Warner.

Case, whose earlier purchases include Internet service provider CompuServe Interactive Services Inc. and also Netscape Communications Corp., a software maker and Web portal, takes only calculated risks. He said AOL's merger with Time Warner was just another milestone in changing interactive services from science fiction into a tool people use each day.

"It's really about enhancing the way people can live their lives," he said.

Case got his first glimpse of the online world in 1982 when he bought a computer for his home. He'd read Alvin Toffler's *The Third Wave* in 1980 and become fascinated by the future of computers.

Back then there was no Internet. "[Linking with other computers] was hard, and the [online] services weren't very compelling," he said.

But Case was still captivated.

"It struck me as magical that I could be sitting at a desk and getting information and talking to people all over the world," he said.

While Case was mulling over the online world, he shifted jobs. In the early 1980s, he moved from working as a brand manager for Procter & Gamble Co. to designing pizza toppings for Pizza Hut Inc.

Case, however, had discovered a passion for technology. In 1985 he decided to go with what excited him. Together with partners Jim Kimsey and Mark Seriff, Case co-founded Quantum Computer Services, a company that produced online software for computer makers. Six years later, the company changed its name to America Online and began selling its service directly to consumers.

Early on, Case decided AOL's service would have to be cutting edge but also easy to use.

"To me, it was less about technology and more about consumers. I always viewed it through the prism of how people would use these services and how they might integrate them in their lives," he said.

Case had to overcome a few obstacles.

AOL's biggest competitor, Prodigy Communications Corp., had vowed to spend $1 billion to market its service. Founded by IBM Corp. and Sears, Roebuck & Co., Prodigy spent millions on TV ads.

AOL had only $1 million in venture funding. So Case tried a new strategy — the company mailed its Internet start-up disks to homes and record stores and struck deals with airlines to distribute disks to passengers. It also advertised online, which was far cheaper than on television.

"Steve had the advantage of not having any money, so there were a lot of innovative approaches," joked Frank Caufield, general partner with venture capital firm Kleiner Perkins Caufield & Byers, an early AOL investor. Caufield has been an AOL board member for 10 years.

The young AOL kept adding subscribers. It also added proprietary services that produced a sense of community for its users.

As AOL's membership grew, so did talk of selling the company. Case balked and hurriedly talked the board out of it, says Nextel's Akerson.

"Steve remained true to his conviction. He has a maniacal belief in his vision. He won't listen to the marginal thinker, and I would argue that it has served him well," Akerson said.

Not that Case has done everything right. In the mid-1990s, AOL allowed subscribers unlimited access to the Internet for a fixed price. The strategy worked too well. Millions of subscribers overran AOL. Many couldn't get online. Piles of bad press reports and consumer lawsuits followed before the company fixed the problems.

The snafus bothered Case.

"The part that was the hardest on me was that I spent more than a decade to get people to trust us, and when they couldn't connect, I knew we were letting them down," he said.

Still, Case was undaunted. He says perseverance is the key when the going gets tough. "You've got to keep your eye on the ball. The bottom line is: Even when people were being critical of us, we were still adding millions of customers every year."

Despite the millions of subscribers and thousands of employees, Case tried to stay close to his customers. He sent out an e-mail to subscribers every month. At the time of the merger, AOL had 7,000 employees dedicated to fielding customer inquiries.

"We are always trying to be good listeners and do a better job at the things that people like and improve the things that people don't like," he said.

Flexibility is vital, and Case changed his management strategy over the years. In the early days, he was involved with every segment of the company. As the company grew, Case learned to delegate more. He no longer attended every single meeting. "In the last five years, I recognized that in order to build a company that we wanted to build, it really required hiring great people and pointing them in the right direction, so I actually tried to figure out as much as possible what things I don't have to do," he said.

Case believes Internet companies should take care not to underestimate the value of employees.

"The companies that are able to attract the best people are going to be the winners in the new century," he said.

Because the Internet is changing so fast, AOL advises employees not to become overconfident. Competition is increasing in the industry, Case says.

"Having a balance between optimism on one hand and paranoia on the other is important," he said. "You want people to be confident without being arrogant."

Case owned roughly $1 billion of stock in AOL in 2000.

For all of his success, though, Case tried to keep the common touch, often dining on turkey sandwiches in AOL's cafeteria.

In January 2000, Case's photo was splashed on the cover of several monthly magazines. So much wealth and attention would be too much for some. Case just shrugged it off. He has a remedy to avoid becoming too self-absorbed.

"The best antidote is not taking things too seriously," he said.

40

Gap Inc. CEO Mickey Drexler

His Focus Made Customer Service
More Than A Slogan

In a business world where shoot-from-the-cuff messaging and canned letters pass for communication, Millard "Mickey" Drexler prefers more substantial contact. He likes to buttonhole people.

That way, he's sure they hear him, and they know he's listening to them. For that reason he loves face-to-face discussions and the phone but hates e-mail and memos.

One of Drexler's first actions when he was hired as president of The Gap stores division of Gap Inc. in 1983 was to fire all the people in the complaint department because they took six weeks to respond. Every employee became the complaint department, and customers occasionally heard directly from Drexler by phone.

Take David Robinson, a lecturer at the Haas School of Business at the University of California at Berkeley. Robinson didn't expect any response when he sent a routine thank-you note for the company's help with one of his courses. Drexler called to invite the whole class to come to his office to chat for a couple of hours about the challenges of retailing.

The students were awed, but from Drexler's standpoint, he was the lucky one — he got a chance to pick their brains about the real world to which he markets. Gap Inc. headquarters in San Francisco is no ivory tower.

By the year 2000, Drexler had built the company into a clothing retailer with $9 billion a year in sales by making customer service more than a slogan on the wall. "Think and act like the customer" is Gap

Inc.'s operating method. To do it successfully, however, requires a unique approach.

The company uses vigorous two-way communication between customers and the staff at the stores of all three chains it operates (The Gap, Banana Republic, Old Navy), and between employees and management.

Drexler set the communication example by being open to comments from everyone.

"He is always talking to people in the stores, in the elevator," said John Wilson, Gap's chief operating officer from 1998 to 2000. "He'll go out and talk to a 12-year-old in the street."

The result? The company is recognized as one of the best-managed apparel retailers.

To stay in closer touch with employees, Drexler started phoning while on his treadmill at home at 6:30 a.m. No one up yet? He left lengthy voice mails (which no one could claim must have been lost in cyberspace).

Instead of spending hours in meetings, Drexler preferred to talk to colleagues in hallways. That way he found out what was going on right then and could give his response immediately.

Drexler learned many of his work habits from his father while growing up in the Bronx. His father was a buyer of buttons and textiles for a coat maker, and they worked together in the Garment District on weekends, holidays and during the summer. He saw his dad's fierce attention to detail and watched the business grow. The younger Drexler developed a taste for his father's focused ways.

He decided he'd need to understand more about running a business. In college, he studied business, devouring texts about sales. During the summers, Drexler worked at the Abraham & Straus department store, where he says he "fell in love with the business." After earning an MBA at Boston University in 1968, the then-23-year-old Drexler became a buyer at Macy's. Showing a flair for merchandising, he next moved to Bloomingdale's. But he wanted more of a challenge.

When the president's spot opened up at the Ann Taylor Stores Corp. clothing chain in 1980, he was picked for it. Once he had the position, he started making changes at the struggling company. As Ann Taylor started to turn around, Gap Inc. founder Don Fischer liked what he saw and was able to hire Drexler away to head The Gap in 1983 when Ann Taylor changed hands.

Gap Inc. needed a turnaround badly. The company had 550 stores. The Gap stores were filled with upscale clothes that weren't selling. It had such a confusing management system that no one could explain its organization. Banana Republic was then mainly a catalog dealer.

Drexler decided he'd have to start over from the bottom. He fired half the regional managers, half the merchandise distributors and half the New York buyers. He began a $10 million renovation of outlets.

He'd always loved to wear simple clothing — and so did just about everyone he knew. Why not make simple casual clothing — clothing people wanted to wear — chic?

Drexler trusted his gut instinct — after all, it led him into a career he was passionate about.

He set up an in-house design department to come up with classic-looking, well-made clothes that had enough flair to appeal to trendy folks' idea of fun. Then he directed the advertising department to focus on that message. With the company's close control of distribution, no other retailers could steal The Gap's ideas before consumers saw them.

Drexler priced clothes moderately, so that even teen-agers could afford them.

The public responded enthusiastically. By mid-2000, the company expected to have more than 3,000 stores. Three years later, it had 4,250.

"We like to think we invented casual Friday," Drexler has quipped. The Gap clothes reflect his personally unpretentious style. As of 2000, Drexler hadn't worn a suit or tie himself to work in 20 years, believing formal dress codes clog creativity and communication.

That doesn't mean he or the company is laid back. Drexler noticed everything down to thread counts and button colors. He tested the clothing, asking people repeatedly about details such as how garments felt, whether they bunched up or were missing some design element.

"Part of [The Gap] culture is about never being satisfied [with achievement]," said Maggie Gross, the company's former director of advertising, "like laboring over the buttons and the stitches — we labor over the way the ads look, the tone, the paper."

Drexler knew customers' first exposure to the chain's clothing was its window displays, so he critiqued them constantly. Display plans were sent out nationally so that every outlet could carry the same message.

To make customers comfortable, he made sure store signs were clear and informative. Staff members were trained to refold immediately any items customers messed up in their search for what they wanted. Employees were told to offer to help customers within 30 seconds after they entered a department. Drexler ordered stores refurbished every seven years to keep them looking fresh.

He reasserted his control and revived the traditional Gap image after a soul-searching period in 1996. Growth in same-store sales had been falling since double-digit gains in 1991 and was flat in 1995, the year he became chief executive of Gap Inc. The company had started to drift from its casual classic market — even employing a two-month punk advertising campaign in 1996. Drexler stepped in and scrapped it.

The financial picture wasn't bleak, but Drexler looked at the figures and realized he wanted more. The Gap was getting $23 out of the $700 spent per capita by Americans on clothing each year, a healthy 3.3% of the market. To Drexler's mind, however, that was just a start.

"Great brands usually dominate a much larger percent of market share than any apparel company does," Drexler said. He decided Gap Inc. should have a much bigger share of the customer's wardrobe.

Toward that end, he put in place a much wider range of sizes stocked so that almost anyone can find something that fits. He dreaded running out of anything, and his idea of a minimum order was what many staff members thought should be the maximum.

In 2002, Mickey Drexler retired as CEO of Gap Inc. after 19 years of company service.

41

Starbucks' Howard Schultz

Keeping His Passion As Fresh As The Morning Coffee

When stress mounts, Howard Schultz digs his hands into a bin of freshly roasted coffee beans and takes a deep whiff.

That strong aroma — the same one that wafted through Starbucks' first crowded espresso bar in Seattle — revives Schultz's original passion for the business, even on bad days.

"It helps me remember how we got started and what we need to sustain," said Schultz, chairman and chief global strategist of Starbucks' Corp. "You have to go back to the cause — which in our case is the coffee. It's our love of coffee."

It's a weekly, if not daily, rite. And it's one of the main reasons Schultz's office is just 20 yards from the tasting room and its bins of beans.

Schultz said he learned the importance of having a trick to count on to rekindle passion as he watched the decay of the British pop band the Beatles. As the Fab Four grew more popular, "They could no longer hear their own music," he said. "They forgot what they stood for."

Following his nose has worked for Schultz, who put together the group of investors that bought out the original Starbucks owners. The then-34-year-old Schultz became president and chief executive of the newly organized chain in 1987. He's built it from one Seattle coffeehouse into today's market leader.

Starbucks introduced mainstream America to Europe's romance with gourmet coffee. Ten years after coming public in 1992, Starbucks had grown to 5,689 stores in 28 countries. In that same period, sales grew an average 20% a year, and profits averaged a 30% annual growth rate. It has the highest customer return rate of any retailer, Schultz said in 1999 — customers come back an average of 18 times a month.

From 1994 to 1999, sales grew at an average annual clip of 49%, and earnings were up an average of 44%. And it has been performing even in the shaky economy of the early 21st century. In 2002, Starbucks had a revenue growth of 24% and net earnings of $215.1 million, the highest reported net earnings in the company's history.

But sniffing coffee isn't Schultz's only secret. Here are six others:

- **Arrive an hour early for critical meetings.** When you get there, walk around the block of the building where you'll be giving the presentation and practice your talk. While walking through crowds, deliver it over and over to yourself. Think you've got it down? Practice again.

  It's worked like a charm for Schultz.

  In 1986, he needed to raise money to keep Il Giornale, his first coffeehouse, in business. (Il Giornale later bought Starbucks Coffee Co.) Schultz had eaten most of his seed money and had already been turned down by several investors.

  His last chance was a meeting with the men known as the "Big Three," investors Jack Benaroya, Herman Sarkowsky and Sam Stroum.

  "I had made my pitch almost a hundred times, but I practiced it again and again before the crucial meeting," Schultz wrote in *Pour Your Heart into It.* "I had to walk around the block three times to calm myself."

  After hearing his talk, the "Big Three" invested $750,000.

- **Speak, don't read, in public.** This goes for any speech, be it the audience, workers, bankers or peers, Schultz says. Even if you think you're a talented orator, you'll sound canned and passionless if you read a speech, he says.

  Afraid you'll forget what to say? So was Schultz until he found the answer: Write three or four words on a 3-by-5-inch index card before the speech.

"These [words] remind me to stay on point of what I want to talk about," he said. "Be sure to include reminders of relevant stories."

"I tell stories people can connect to," Schultz said. "People are hungry for human contact and to be attached to a cause through something they can relate to."

- **Beware of hiring people from bureaucratic companies.** When you hire workers, you're hiring more than their labor. You're also hiring the baggage they bring from the company or companies they used to work for, Schultz says.

  "I would not [rule out] someone because they come from a bureaucratic company," he said. "But I would be more skeptical and more probing to see if that person can escape that culture."

- **Be vulnerable.** Schultz has cried not only in front of his son but also in front of workers. He's been open about things that worry him. He's so open that people often tell him, "Howard, I can't believe you were that vulnerable."

  Schultz doesn't see that as a weakness. Just the opposite. There's no better way to show your honesty than by showing your fears, he says. And honesty with workers and customers is one of the top ingredients of success.

  "People are hungry to be touched by the authenticity of people they can believe in," he said.

  Talk about honesty. The 1995 Christmas season was a nightmare for Starbucks. It was stuck with a glut of expensive beans that it bought when prices were rising. Consumers — looking for traditional red-and-green-wrapped gifts — weren't buying into Starbucks stylish but pastel-colored ones.

  Schultz kept his worries inside for weeks and kept a smile on his face. But as December wore on, he changed his tactics. He called all the Seattle-based workers into a room on the third floor at headquarters. There he admitted to them what they already knew: We're having a disappointing holiday season.

It was then that Schultz learned an important lesson. "When the chips are down, it's wrong to give a rah-rah Knute Rockne speech," he wrote. "I believe that if you level with your employees in bad times, they will trust you more when you say things are going well."

- **Be upbeat.** Although Schultz doesn't candy-coat bad news, he says that leaders must be optimistic. "Leaders have an intuitive sense that things will work out for the best," he said. "I do not see the dark side."

  Schultz learned the perks of positive thinking growing up in the public housing projects of Canarsie in Brooklyn. His father supported a family of five without ever making more than $20,000 a year. "I literally grew up on the other side of the tracks — no one gave me anything," Schultz said.

  But Schultz's mother taught him to stay optimistic. "My mother . . . was able to instill in me a self-esteem that convinced me that I had the ability to do things beyond the abyss we found ourselves in.

  "I willed [success] to happen. I took my life in my hands, learned from anyone I could, grabbed what opportunity I could and molded my success step by step," Schultz wrote.

  Schultz still assumes going into any situation that he'll win. And that gives him the courage to take chances.

  "I've learned you must put yourself in a position to win," Schultz said.

- **Build on memorable experiences by reading.** After returning from an "important spiritual experience in Israel last summer, I wanted to keep it alive," Schultz said. So he read *The Haj*, a story of man's spiritual journey in the Middle East written by Leon Uris.

  After a trip to Japan in 1998, Schultz read *Memoirs of a Geisha* by Arthur Golden. And after visiting the Franklin Delano Roosevelt memorial in Washington,

D.C., Schultz read four biographies on the Depression-era president.

The busier Schultz gets, the more he reads, he says. He reads "voraciously" on airplanes, packing two or three books with him to make sure he doesn't run out.

When Schultz reads something top-notch — such as *Orbiting the Giant Hairball* by Gordon MacKenzie — he orders hundreds of extra copies and hands them out to workers.

"The book talks — metaphorically — of making sure you don't let bureaucracy stand in your way," said Schultz, who handed out 500 copies of it to employees in 1998.

In April 2000, Schultz appointed business partner and longtime friend Orin Smith as Starbucks' new CEO and himself as the company's chief global strategist.

42

IBM's Linda Sanford
Her Attention To Detail Put Her On The Fast Track

Flipping through stacks of résumés, Linda Sanford sees it all. IBM wannabes boldface their Ivy League degrees and gigs at hot Internet start-ups.

But those aren't the things that most impress Sanford, one-time general manager of IBM Corp.'s Global Industries group, the computer company's biggest unit.

What does? Sanford looks for people who have scooped ice cream — even as teen-agers.

"I look for people who have had jobs that kept them in front of customers . . . like working in an ice-cream store," Sanford said. "Those are the people who will come up with IBM's next big idea." Forget what career counselors have told you about deleting high school jobs from your résumé, Sanford says. When studying résumés, she looks at those jobs first. "Jobs early in a person's career show [the candidate's] natural instincts."

Sanford's attention to details helps explain her fast rise within IBM. Within 25 years at IBM, Sanford rose from a spot as a typewriter engineer to the head of the company's $24.8 billion Global Industries unit.

Global Industries has been IBM's secret pearl. While it accounts for 70% of IBM's yearly revenue, it doesn't appear on financial statements. Why not? The Armonk, N.Y.–based computer company breaks results down by products, not by customers. And Global Industries oversees sales to entire industry groups.

How did Sanford rise through the ranks so fast? Here are some of her other tips:

- **When you're ready to make a decision, always ask one more question.** Forcing yourself to come up with one last query brings out fears lurking in the back of your mind, Sanford says.

  Sanford learned this the hard way. Before approving the design for a new inkjet printer, something irked her. She noticed that the paint on the European model's plastic housing was different from that to be used in the U.S. model.

  She squelched her concerns. After all, she'd studied the printer's design from top to bottom. Everything looked fine.

  Too bad she didn't ask the question. Just before the printers were made, it was found that the U.S. model's paint didn't meet flammability standards. Luckily, the error was caught before it was too late.

  "I saw the materials were different, but I didn't ask why," Sanford said. "It bothered me . . . how could I have missed?"

  Instead of dwelling on the problem, she learned a lesson she'll never forget: Not admitting to a mistake is worse than making one.

  "If you don't admit a mistake, you won't be better the next time," she said. "Ask yourself what could I have done differently?"

- **Race to save a sinking ship.** Does your company have a struggling department? Is there a sick product line or a team with no morale? That's the project a true leader would crave, Sanford says.

  She'd know. Sanford was assigned to IBM's main-frame business in 1992. It seemed like a career-ending move.

IBM's S/390 mainframes — large and expensive computers used mainly by huge corporations — were headed down the tubes. Companies were replacing their "big iron" with much cheaper personal computers and high-powered servers.

IBM was slow to respond. Thousands of workers suffered from IBM's first-ever layoffs.

"I came in at a time when mainframes had hit the wall. They were considered dinosaurs, the scourge of the earth, dying and extinct," Sanford said.

Rather than worry, Sanford got busy. "You learn a lot more from near-death experiences than you do when you take over a well-running ship."

What'd she do? First, she had to make sure that workers had positive attitudes. To do this, she started walking, literally. She strolled up and down workers' cubicles in the company's offices in Poughkeepsie, N.Y., Germany and France. She knocked on customers' doors.

From time to time, she'd stop to see what workers were doing and talk about their ideas. She'd ask them questions: What are your concerns? Why do you think the unit isn't successful right now? How can we save the unit?

After the fact-finding mission, she mobilized. Regular "town hall" meetings were started. Workers in New York were gathered in the lunchroom with a speakerphone connecting the overseas colleagues, also seated in their lunchrooms.

Almost like a fireside chat, those sessions were a chance for Sanford to discuss what she'd learned from her walks. This calmed their worry, so they could focus on improvement.

And they did. In the three years before Sanford was named general manager of the S/390 unit — 1992 to 1994 — the compound annual growth rate of computing power (or MIPS) shipped to customers was a meager 6%. But during her three-year term — 1995 to 1997 — that growth rocketed to 45%.

- **Walk the factory floor.** Put on a hard-hat and get into the plant, Sanford says. Too many managers lock themselves up with white-collar, cubical-dwelling workers. To see what's really going on, talk to the people who put products together and ship them.

  "You can see very quickly how many boxes are being pumped out of the door," she said. "That's the easiest way to see how the business is going."

  Sanford saw something else on the factory floor.

  Once she asked to look at a factory worker's computer. She scrolled through screens expecting to see the standard things — online product testing programs and schedules of upcoming jobs. But she found more.

  This worker had put hotlinks to Web sites that tracked current events that could affect IBM's mainframe sales. There were also links to rivals' Web sites. When looking around more, Sanford found all the workers had similar Web links.

  "Just seeing that told me the people — from the factory-floor on up — were committed to the business," she said. "Their wanting to know [these details] told me we could pull out of this."

- **Look for creative ways to discuss problems.** Sanford called a two-day meeting in a hotel in White Plains, N.Y. It was for IBM's 500 female workers in technical areas to get to know each other.

  "As large as 500 may sound, it gets diluted when you look at [the fact that] 270,000 people work at IBM," she said.

  How'd she get the workers to open up? She conducted "poster sessions." Participants are given crayons and magic markers and asked to fill white poster board signs with pictures of problems they're working on.

  Attendees then took turns walking around, looking at the posters and asking the "artists" about their work.

  "We got fantastic feedback," Sanford said. "Many people told me this is the best they'd ever seen at IBM."

- **Know your customer, at any cost.** Readers of Dale Carnegie books know this: To win someone over, be interested in what's on their mind.

  So she's shocked at how many salespeople still try to jam products down customers' throats.

  Sanford is using computers to fix this. Under her suggestion, all salespeople have a system loaded on their laptops.

  When they turn on their computers — before leaving their hotels on sales calls — salespeople get a screen full of things their customers might be worried about. The customer's competition, news and even past orders flash up on the screen.

  In minutes, they can scan the data and see what's on their customers' minds.

  Of course, there's no way to make sure salespeople read the screen. But Sanford's not worried. After all — she knows she's hired workers used to dealing with customers — even scooping ice cream.

  "Top employees have one thing in common, they work with customers," she said.

In 2000, Sanford was named senior vice president of IBM Storage System group. She has since been named senior vice president of Enterprise on Demand Transformation, responsible for the internal business transformation of IBM to an on-demand business.

43

99 Cents Only Stores' David Gold

He Ignored Status Quo To Break New Retailing Ground

David Gold's success story reads something like those of other retailers. He works hard, finds and sells products with good value and focuses on serving customers. But the parallels stop there.

When Commerce, Calif.–based 99 Cents Only Stores prepared to come public in May 1996, investment bankers advised Gold to take a higher salary, accept a yearly bonus and receive stock options. Gold refused all three.

The longtime chairman and chief executive told them he felt amply rewarded by the large chunk of shares he owned in the company. In his mind, bonuses and options for him would only cut earnings and dilute shareholder value.

To make his company grow in the healthiest way, he knew he'd need dedicated, loyal employees. So Gold decided instead to award options to every member of the 99 Cents team.

"The one thing that gratifies our family the most is that every single employee of the company gets stock options after six months, whether they're part time or full time," said the then-68-year-old Gold in a 2000 interview. The firm granted options worth 985,444 shares to employees in 1999.

No options went to Gold; his two sons, Howard and Jeff, who are both vice presidents; or Eric Schiffer, the firm's president and

Gold's son-in-law. The options hold the potential to enrich each employee, and they also inspire a companywide drive to succeed.

"Your management believes the options help to reduce turnover and theft and motivate stockers and cashiers with management potential to become management trainees," the firm's latest annual report said. Gold's refusal to follow the crowd has helped him pioneer the concept of selling items at one price into a major force in the retail industry. Started in 1982, 99 Cents Only Stores is the nation's oldest existing single-price retailer. Within 20 years, it grew into a chain of 150 company-owned stores in southern and central California, Nevada and Arizona.

Gold has never raised prices at his stores, but that hasn't stunted the firm's growth. Earnings rose an average of 32% every year from 1995 to 2000. Sales tripled from $123 million in 1993 to $360 million in 1999. Sales averaged $4.8 million per store in 2002, and new store return on investment exceeded 99%.

Before launching 99 Cents, Gold and his wife, Sherry, ran a successful liquor shop during the 1960s inside bustling Grand Central Market in downtown Los Angeles. Keeping a keen eye on sales trends, Gold found that sales dropped fast when he hiked the price of an item from 99 cents to $1.09. He also found that items sold better at 99 cents than at 98 cents.

That observation got him thinking. Why not open a store in which every item would always sell at the same price?

Yet Gold knew that building a business based on that concept alone wasn't enough. He had to find ways to create a new shopping experience that other chains hadn't offered.

Retailing executives and shoppers saw deep-discount stores as dark, messy warehouselike places where a customer didn't expect clean floors or neat, orderly shelves. Gold decided to buck conventional wisdom by keeping his stores clean and making them visually appealing.

Gold makes sure that lighting inside each 99 Cents store is unusually bright. Rows of long fluorescent lights, four bulbs in each row, span the ceilings just several feet apart. White-painted walls enhance the brightness. He also makes sure shelves are no more than 5 feet tall so that shoppers can see almost everything from any spot in the store.

Often, deep-discount stores have no windows — or only small windows — facing the street. They look less like stores and more like fortresses.

Gold makes his shops stand out by installing huge windows in each storefront. He fills them with sharp rows of name-brand consumer items with brightly colored packaging — from aluminum wrap to name-brand detergent to imported chocolate.

The window displays serve as free advertising and create a visual rainbow effect that draws passersby into the store.

"We never copied anyone else," Gold said.

To offer the best possible service, Gold tries to think like a customer. He remembers the time as a youth when the cashier at the local May Co. department store refused to serve his family at 8:55 p.m. because the store was going to close five minutes later.

Store hours at the 99 Cents outlets are from 9 to 9. But Gold has his managers let people come in and shop a few minutes before opening time and walk down the aisles a few minutes after closing.

"He is a true merchant," said Macon Brock Jr., president and chief executive of Chesapeake, Va.–based Dollar Tree Stores Inc., a rival and the country's largest single-price retail chain in 2000.

When Gold's venture started, most people doubted they could buy high-quality goods for under a buck. Gold set out to prove otherwise.

He looked for good merchandise, stalking deals at close-outs. He consistently offered customers the best of what he found.

He built a strong reputation as a reliable purchaser. Each 99 Cents store carries thousands of items, including many name-brand consumables. Gold says his stores buy directly from every major U.S. manufacturer.

To develop strong relationships with suppliers, Gold has never made a late payment. He's also never canceled a purchase order.

"Quite often we would agree to buy an order of glassware from one supplier during one of our open buying sessions [at the company headquarters]. Then 20 minutes later, someone shows up with a better glass," Gold said. "We will never cancel the first order, but we might also buy the second one."

Some suppliers will show up with just a few cases, or far less than what was agreed on. Gold will still honor the deal. Alternatively, a supplier could arrive with hundreds more cases than expected. Again, he'll accept the entire shipment and pay for all of it. He figures that he'll be able to find the right way to sell it.

The basic rule at company headquarters? "Treat people the way you would like to be treated," Gold said.

Take the time several years ago when a supplier shipped Gold a bigger-than-expected amount of items. Gold called the supplier to report what happened.

The supplier's chief later noted at an industry conference that was the first time anyone had called about an overshipment. The manufacturer discovered it'd been placing too many items on each pallet at the warehouse and was overshipping to all its customers.

Some suppliers restrict 99 Cents from advertising certain products, especially those that normally sell for several dollars wholesale and are found at other chains. So Gold found creative ways to use his company's name to spread word about his stores.

At every store's grand opening, nine 19-inch color televisions are sold at 99 cents apiece. The next nine customers can buy one of nine microwave ovens — again for 99 cents each.

The long lines that grow days before a store's opening make splashes in local media. Gold has held the same color-television promotion for each store since the chain started. He keeps trying new ways to garner attention for his stores. When George Burns turned 99, for instance, the company ran full-page newspaper ads congratulating the cigar-smoking comedian. And on April Fools' Day, 99 Cents Only runs ads of items selling at $99 each.

44

Entrepreneur
Madame C. J. Walker
She Used Marketing Savvy And
Determination To Win Customers

Madame C. J. Walker was horrified. She was 37, and her hair was falling out. If she couldn't stop it soon, she knew she'd face baldness.

As an American black woman at the turn of the century, Walker (1867–1919) knew she wasn't alone; hair loss was one of the inevitable results of the poor diet many black women had. But she also saw that not everyone in her community suffered the same problem. She had to figure out a way to halt the hair loss.

She searched for a remedy, trying all kinds of available potions and homemade remedies. None was completely successful.

Finally, after long experimentation, she found a pomade invented by the Poro Co.'s Annie N. Turnbo Malone that worked. Yet it still wasn't quite right, Walker thought.

Rather than reinvent the wheel, she added several secret vitamins and minerals and waited. Slowly, her hair began to return to its original thickness.

A domestic servant with no chance for advancement, Walker — who was born Sarah Breedlove in Louisiana — knew she wanted a job that would allow her to be financially independent. What if she could sell her solution to other people?

She dubbed her product the Wonderful Hair Grower and began mapping out her marketing strategy. In a few years, Walker's efforts would not only revolutionize personal sales and the beauty market for black women but also make her the first woman millionaire in America.

Walker, who based her business in Indianapolis, knew she wanted to reach as many black women as possible. Yet many of them couldn't read. That ruled out advertisements.

She also knew that not many blacks trusted white people. She couldn't just have white salesmen hawk her product to local stores — it might be rejected out of hand.

Her friends had all tried the product and, in turn, recommended it to their other friends. Why not use that face-to-face network to sell her invention?

So Walker decided to operate her business completely by black women for black women. No one had ever attempted such a thing.

She assessed the situation; she had little capital. As the child of slaves, she was at the bottom of the social and financial strata. Her risk was very small; the upside potential seemed unlimited.

"Adversity teaches you a great deal about survival skills," said David Ford, professor of management and leadership development at the University of Texas, Dallas. "Being free from the fear of failure was a great thing for her."

Marketing was still a primitive science in her day, and companies used high-pressure sales tactics to move goods that people often had no need for. Walker recognized that those tactics wouldn't help her succeed.

Instead of hawking her hair grower like a snake-oil salesman, she tailored her product and distribution network to her customers. She identified the needs of black women as different from the needs of white women.

She believed firmly in selling by example. She insisted on "cleanliness and loveliness" for all her saleswomen, who were called "Walker agents." Their neatly arranged hair, black skirts and white blouses served a dual purpose: In addition to making them easily recognizable as they moved through neighborhoods, the uniforms and sparkling hygiene gave the agents additional self-confidence.

Customers were enthralled by the sales method and enthusiastically bought the hair grower.

They weren't the only ones happy with the results. At a time when most black women performed menial labor, the agents became a visible ray of hope within the community. Walker's agents were quickly enriched by their efforts. Some earned up to $1,000 per day.

"C. J. Walker carved out and created a legacy of African-American participation in the hair- and beauty-care industries," said Charles Murphy, an associate professor of business at Howard University in Washington, D.C. "If she lived today, she would probably still be successful."

Walker realized that economic emancipation was the only way for black women to break the cycle of discrimination, poverty and economic abuse. By giving her agents sizable commissions, she understood that she could, in effect, motivate them the same way she'd motivated herself.

"I am a woman who came from the cotton fields of the South. I was promoted from there to the washtub," Walker said. "Then I was promoted to the cooks' kitchen, and from there I promoted myself."

Although Walker was a savvy entrepreneur, she was illiterate when she established her business, making expansion a difficult endeavor.

She sent her daughter, Lelia, to college so that at least one member of the family would be educated. She was so impressed by the change in Lelia that she established Lelia College, a cosmetology school for training and educating all Walker agents.

To ensure she wouldn't get fleeced, Walker surrounded herself with educated people to assist her in business.

While traveling, she met a black man named Freeman B. Ransom who had a law degree but worked as a train porter. Walker hired him on the spot and put him in charge of plant operations, giving her the freedom to stay in personal contact with her agents in the field.

She also recognized that she needed to educate herself. So Walker employed tutors to teach her to read and write. Her commitment to education stayed with her, and she became a major supporter of education for black women.

Walker put the stamp of her character and personality on everything that she did. Never quitting and boldly staring down failure were instilled in all Walker agents.

"She had one of the characteristics that a lot of successful business people have," Ford said. "In the face of great obstacles, they never give up."

45

Master Of Advertising
David Ogilvy
He Built On Quality

D avid Ogilvy had a simple formula for attracting new clients: Do good work for old ones.

The easiest way to get new clients is to do good advertising, Ogilvy wrote in his seminal work, *Ogilvy on Advertising.*

"During one period of seven years, we never failed to win an account for which we competed, and all I did was show the campaigns we had created. Sometimes I did not even have to do that. One afternoon, a man walked into my office without an appointment and gave me the IBM account; he knew our work."

Client by client, Ogilvy (1911–99) built up his ad agency, Ogilvy & Mather.

Even when he became extremely successful — *Advertising Age* magazine called him one of the most widely known "creative gods" in advertising history — he didn't take anything for granted.

He made promoting his agency one of his most important duties. He scheduled at least two major speeches a year, each carefully staged and crafted for maximum impact, according to *Ad Age.*

Also, he befriended researchers, public relations people, management consultants and sales reps because he knew they were in constant contact with potential clients. He also included periodic Ogilvy & Mather progress reports sent to 600 people.

Ogilvy was born in West Horsley, England, and sought from a young age to climb his way up the ladder. Though he attended Christ Church College at Oxford University, he was eager to try his hand in the business world. He left Oxford and went to Paris, where he worked in the kitchen of the Hotel Majestic. Feeling like he had some experience under his belt, he returned to England and went to work for Aga Cookers selling stoves door to door.

More Than Quantity

One of the lessons learned during this period: Making a large number of sales calls alone isn't enough.

The more prospects you talk to, the more sales you expose yourself to, the more orders you will get, he wrote. But never mistake quantity of calls for quality of salesmanship.

To help others learn, Ogilvy wrote a guide for Aga salesmen that *Fortune* magazine called probably the best sales manual ever written.

Wanting to build his sales skills, Ogilvy worked briefly for Aga's ad agency, Mather & Crowther. Yet he wanted more. Seeing more opportunity in the U.S., he moved here in 1938. He went to work for George Gallup's Audience Research Institute, where he learned the importance of research to find out what your customers want.

"If you cannot afford the service of professionals to do this research, do it yourself. Informal conversations with half a dozen housewives can sometimes help, more than formal surveys," Ogilvy wrote.

Ogilvy considered it important to know the product inside and out. First study the product you're going to advertise. The more you know about it, the more likely you'll come up with a big idea for selling it.

When Ogilvy landed the Rolls-Royce account, he spent three weeks reading about the car and came across a statement that at 60 miles an hour, the loudest noise comes from an electric clock. That became the headline of one of Ogilvy's most famous ads.

He thought it important to know what the competition does regarding similar products. Imagine what a client would feel if he found out his brand-new campaign has a twin sister, he wrote.

During World War II, Ogilvy worked for the British Secret Service, writing reports and analyzing data on matters of diplomacy and security. After the war he bought a farm in Pennsylvania, but it took just a few years to recognize that farming wasn't his forte.

So he returned to what he did well: selling. But what agency would hire an unemployed college dropout who knew nothing about marketing? To make it worse, he'd never written an ad in his life.

Time to strike out on his own, Ogilvy figured. Relying on the force of personality and determination, he persuaded his former employers at Mather & Crowther to back him. In 1948 he founded Hewitt, Ogilvy, Benson & Mather, which eventually became O&M.

As the agency grew and opened offices around the world, Ogilvy made it a habit to always send a gift to anyone appointed to head an office. It was a Russian doll that had smaller and smaller dolls inside each one. In the smallest, Ogilvy placed a note and hiring advice. The note said:

> If each of us hires people who are smaller than we are, we shall become a company of dwarves. But if each of us hires people bigger than we are, Ogilvy & Mather will become a company of giants.

Ogilvy prized individuality and confidence in his employees. People who needed the support of committees weren't likely to be hired. A lot of advertisements and television commercials look like minutes of a committee meeting, and that is what they are, Ogilvy said. Advertising seems to sell most when a solitary individual writes it. He must study the product, the research and the precedents. Then he must shut the door of his office and write the advertisements.

As he wrote in *Confessions of an Advertising Man*, "Search all your parks in all your cities. You'll find no statues of committees."

The more intrigued people were, the more they'd buy, Ogilvy believed. You can't bore people into buying.

He also believed that creativity came even within the parameters of discipline. Shakespeare wrote his sonnets within a strict discipline — 14 lines of iambic pentameter rhyming in three quatrains and a couplet. Were his sonnets dull? Mozart wrote sonatas within an equally rigid discipline. Were they dull?

Ads Sold As They Should

Ogilvy pushed for ads that were written in everyday language. At the time the campaign was introduced, a minor controversy raged over the slogan "Winston tastes good, like a cigarette should." Grammatically, that should've read, "Winston tastes good, as a cigarette should."

Ogilvy dismissed the critics as insufferable pedants and, according to *Advertising Age* magazine, added: "If you're trying to persuade people to do something or buy something, it seems to me you should use the language they use every day."

Ogilvy drew on his experience as a manager. One of the principles that guided him came from when he worked at the Hotel Majestic, when the chef occasionally left his desk and menu planning behind to work in the kitchen.

"A crowd of us always gathered around to watch, spellbound by his virtuosity," Ogilvy wrote in *Confessions*. "It was inspiring to work for a supreme master."

46

Cisco Systems' John Chambers

He Makes Sure The Customer Is
Always First

John Chambers knows within five minutes whether the company he's thinking of buying is the right fit.

"I can walk into another CEO's office, who we're looking at acquiring, and I can tell by how their office is set up and the first five minutes of conversation . . . and decide on the probability of whether or not there's a match," Chambers said.

It's that kind of acquisition savvy that Chambers has used to push computer networking player Cisco Systems Inc. to the top. In the first five years after Chambers became chief executive in late 1994, the San Jose, Calif.–based concern made 44 acquisitions. 2001 sales exceeded $22 billion, up more than 120 times fiscal 1991 sales of $183 million.

Exactly what does the sharp-eyed Chambers look for when he visits the target company's CEO?

"I look at the size of the office," he said. "Mine's 11-by-12-by-12 [feet]. [At Cisco] the employees are out where the light is, and the managers are more towards the middle. We look at what the people have in their office. I have plain furniture. There isn't mahogany anywhere."

To get a better picture of the culture, the Cisco CEO also studies how stock options are distributed at the target company.

"If they're all spread out over the management and not spread throughout the company, it says a lot about the culture of the company and the leader," Chambers said.

He even looks at the walls.

"You can tell by what they have on the wall what's important to them in life," Chambers said. "You look for pictures of their family, the commonality of pictures of sports, coaches and things like that."

Heeds Details

It's such attention to detail that makes Chambers a strong leader, says John Morgridge, Cisco's CEO from 1988 to 1994 and chairman since 1995. He recommended the then-44-year-old Chambers for the CEO job.

Chambers was named CEO in late 1994 after being a senior vice president since 1991.

"He's certainly met and exceeded my expectations," Morgridge said.

How does he do it? Chambers likens himself to a coach. He needs to pick the right team to be successful.

"What I'm after is a teamwork mentality and people who like to compete," Chambers said. "I like to compete. While I don't like getting beat, if you play well, that's OK. I'd rather play well and get beat than not play at all or beat somebody who's not very good."

He follows a rigorous process to find such employees.

"First we look at people who've had a consistent record of overachieving," Chambers said. "An indication of how well they'll do in the future is how well they've done in the past."

He also wants to know about teams that prospective employees have built.

"I ask them who are the top people they've recruited," Chambers said. "Where are they today? If they stare at you, you have a big problem. The quality of the team determines your winning."

He peppers job candidates with questions about their knowledge of the industry and looks for a spark. "You see it in their eyes if they're really enthusiastic," he said.

He's uncompromising about hiring team players. He listens for "we" instead of "I" in conversation.

"We've let people go who were 125% of their goal but just weren't team players," Chambers said. "They were always focusing on themselves and what was right for them, not the company."

Customer focus, open communication and the ability to balance long- and short-term goals are crucial to the mix, Chambers says.

"Then I go check it with their references, not the references they gave me, but other references within their company who I know," he said.

Chambers knows what makes people tick, Morgridge says. That's why Cisco keeps the majority of the workers from acquisitions, he says.

Cisco's overall attrition rate is 3% a year in an industry that averages 20%, Chambers said in 1999. A mere 6% of employees from acquired companies leave.

"If I can keep them in the first 6 to 12 months, I can probably keep them for the second and third year," Chambers said. "We go over the top management with our board of directors. We know what motivates each one of them. We do our homework."

Money isn't the reason people stay, Chambers says. They want a stimulating place to work, leaders with vision and a higher purpose than a paycheck, he says. Cisco gives them that.

"We outline goals that other people say are impossible, and then we meet them again and again," he said. "We build a culture where this is understood."

To make sure it is, Chambers gives team members the freedom to do their jobs. He doesn't hover.

He also keeps them motivated to win.

When a team succeeds, stock options follow. Regular workers, not just top managers, get stock options. Some 42% of Cisco's non-management staff members received stock options as of 1999. On average, each of those people had more than $250,000 in stock appreciation, he says.

Chambers uses stock options to push his vice presidents to think long term. At the end of the 1990s, he raised their vesting time to five years from four years to force them to think an extra year out.

"You tie the main motivation into the reward system," Chambers said. "If you want them to be team players, you better motivate them on team issues, not individual performance."

Chambers makes sure everyone on the team knows that customer satisfaction is key to a team's success. It even applies to the boss.

Why He Was Late

When Cisco bought GeoTel Communications Corp. for $2 billion in mid-April 1999, Chambers was 15 minutes late to the board meeting.

Why? He was on the phone with a customer.

"He sent a message to the board that said the customer comes first," said Dan Scheinman, Cisco's vice president of legal and government affairs.

Chambers has reason to pay close attention to Cisco customers. They've helped Cisco get ahead of trends. Ford Motor Co. and Boeing Co. officials told him to buy Crescendo Communications Inc., which makes Fast Ethernet gear, back in 1993.

"Boeing was even blunter than that," Chambers said. "They said, 'If you want this $10 million order, you better buy this company.'"

Chambers talks fast and doesn't walk — he runs all day long.

To keep his energy level up for 12- to 18-hour days, he jogs three to five miles several times a week. He also makes use of every second of time.

His morning starts with a 20-minute shower when he plans his day and thinks through the key issues. Next he studies his agenda before leaving for work.

Then Chambers catches up on voice mail on the drive to work, leaving 12 to 25 messages.

"As soon as I get into the office, the first thing I do is to grab a Diet Coke and the [sales] numbers," he said. He even gets the daily sales numbers on the weekend.

Chambers runs at such a fast pace because he knows what can happen if he stumbles.

An eight-year veteran of now-defunct Wang Laboratories Inc., his biggest regret is not pushing Wang to change to making personal computers from minicomputers.

"For 30 years [Wang] was very successful," Chambers said. "That's a lesson I learned: People remember you for how you end up, not all the years of success."

PART 6

Succeeding Through Innovation

eBay Founder Pierre Omidyar

His Devotion To Community Created

A Global Auction House

From tinkering with a hobby to a multibillion-dollar online auction company, Pierre Omidyar, founder and chairman of eBay Inc., made it happen.

He did it by taking a great idea through small progressions and fostering a special and personal community on the Internet. He launched eBay in September 1995. Within months, the auction house became the world's largest and most compelling Internet commerce platform.

In 2000 the company boasted more than 22 million registered users, a community larger than the population of Texas. Netting revenue of $431.4 million in 2000, eBay's total assets reached $1.2 billion.

In April 1999 Omidyar's worth mounted to about $4.8 billion. He held 31.2% of eBay's common stock.

Omidyar created eBay to help his girlfriend trade Pez candy dispensers in the San Francisco Bay area where they lived — the "electronic Bay area." Omidyar hoped the site would serve as a neighborhood community for sellers and buyers to meet.

He called it "Auction Web" at first — his after-work hobby, a site on his personal Web page. His local Internet service provider hosted it for $30 a month. While working as an engineer for General Magic Inc., where he developed the first Web-enabled application for Magic Cap, he noticed the money starting to roll in from his Web page.

At first it was small change taped onto index cards — fees for users to post their goods on the page. It didn't take long for buyers and sellers to discover the opportunity the site gave them to find and sell goods. Within months his ISP insisted he upgrade his service; traffic on the page had grown beyond its capacity.

Astonished by his success, Omidyar acted promptly. He wrote some code and set up a new site devoted to auctions. Still thinking of it as a community-based trading platform, he renamed it eBay and charged sellers who posted an auction notice from 25 cents to $2. He also collected 1.25% to 5% of the value of each final sale on eBay.

Nine months after the first auction, Omidyar quit his day job and focused on eBay. His "neighborhood community" started to encompass the world. In 1997, Benchmark Capital invested $22 million in eBay for a 22% stake and furthered the company's growth.

By the end of 1997, eBay showed sales growth of 1,432.3%.

Omidyar took eBay public in 1998 with an initial public offering price of $18 a share. The company's visibility increased when it secured prominent displays on Netscape's search page along with other major search engines, shopping guides and classifieds.

Its stock has been one of the performers of the bearish early 2000s, ranging from a low of about $50 a share to a high of $90. In 2000, eBay had net revenue of $431.4 million. That number more than doubled in 2002 to $1.21 billion.

As of 2003, eBay features more than 18,000 categories of goods to buy and sell within. About 12 million items can be seen every day, with users adding hundreds of thousands of items daily. In the year 2000 alone, eBay users listed more than 265 million items.

The number of registered users and the number of listings have increased every year since eBay came public in 1997. At the end of that year, there were under 1 million users and about 4 million listings. By the end of 2002, there were 62 million registered users and 195 million listings.

According to Media Metrix, a company that measures Web audience, visitors spend more time on eBay than on any other Web site.

Omidyar enhanced the eBay community over time by adding a chat room, the "eBay café" and the "Feedback Forum," through which users comment on their dealings with each other. In July 2000, eBay acquired Half.com and began set-price trading.

The company makes customer service available 24 hours a day via e-mail. With a system called "SafeHarbor," eBay protects the community from fraud.

Users have not only created second businesses or quit their day jobs to sell their goods on eBay, they've also been known to meet and even marry.

Appointed chairman of eBay in 1998, Omidyar turned day-to-day operations over to Meg Whitman as president and chief executive. eBay thrives under Whitman's guidance; she's expanding eBay's services through site launches in Australia, Canada, Germany, Japan and the United Kingdom, as well as acquisitions and joint ventures.

Today eBay also enables trade locally and internationally in Europe and Asia with a presence in Latin America and China.

Stepping away from the workaday grind with time on his hands and billions of dollars, Omidyar faced a rare question:

"What does a billionaire do with all that money?"

Change the world, of course. After grappling with the complications of aiding good causes, Omidyar started the eBay Foundation in 1998. In just over four years, the foundation made more than $2.9 million in grants to some 75 nonprofit organizations.

The foundation furthers Omidyar's personal goals to apply and teach technology and foster self-sufficiency. The goal: self-improvement for all people and a sense of connection within a global community.

Omidyar knew from the beginning where his talents lay. He was known to sneak out of gym class to play with computers, even writing computer programs. At 14, he wrote his first program for his high school library to catalog books. He studied computer science at Tufts University. After graduating, he developed consumer applications for Claris, a subsidiary of Apple Computer.

In 1991, Omidyar and three friends co-founded Ink Development Corp. He was instrumental in guiding the firm into Internet shopping. That company later renamed itself eShop Inc. Microsoft bought it in 1996, and Omidyar lent his talents to General Magic while developing what would become eBay.

Omidyar was born to Iranian parents in Paris. When his father accepted a residency at Johns Hopkins University Medical Center, the family moved to the U.S. Omidyar married "into a world-class Pez collection" in 1999. He and his wife, Pamela, live in Paris.

In January 2000, Omidyar accepted his first board position outside of eBay. He joined the board of directors of ePeople, an online marketplace for technical support.

48

Innovators
Ole And Bess Evinrude
Their Resolve And Integrity Launched
Millions Of Outboard Motors

It took two people to bring the "detachable rowboat motor" to the masses: one to build it; one to see the potential and sell it. The fact that they were married was just icing on the cake.

Tinkering in his machine shop in Milwaukee in the spring of 1908, Ole Evinrude devised what he saw as a novelty. The motor looked like a coffee grinder, teased his wife, Bess. But what she really saw was dollar signs.

"Hundreds of people will want that motor as soon as they know about it," she said. Ole (1877–1934) pointed out that others had built two similar outboard motors that had failed because they proved more trouble than they were worth.

"Then yours must be reliable," Bess said. "It must be foolproof and trouble proof. If it is a good motor, it will sell," she told him, as she recalled in an interview in *The American Magazine* in February 1928.

After Ole tinkered some more, one of his shop employees took the improved motor to nearby Pewaukee Lake for a test on the back of a rowboat. The excursion netted 10 orders for the "fool novelty."

Ole was pleased. Bess's appetite, on the other hand, was merely whetted. She put every spare penny of Ole's machine pattern-making company's tight budget into advertising.

Ole was the inventor, Bess the one with business sense. They both had the same resolve, ability to overcome setbacks and integrity. Together, they launched what would become the world's largest outboard motor maker.

After the Pewaukee Lake demonstration, Bess sat at the typewriter in her kitchen and wrote a print ad that would change their lives: "Don't row! Throw the oars away! Use an Evinrude Motor."

"A few days after the magazine came out, Ollie (her pet name for Ole) came home looking like a mail carrier. His coat pockets bulged with letters, and both of his hands were full. He dumped those letters onto the table, and we danced a jig around him," Bess recalled.

It was the second time Ole had won over a skeptical audience. The first skeptic was his stern, Norwegian-born father, Andrew. The family moved to America when Ole was 5.

During his Wisconsin adolescence, Ole had tried to build an 18-foot sailboat without letting his father discover it. Andrew, a practical farmer, did find out, however, and cracked the boat pieces over his knee for kindling.

Undaunted, Ole started again, this time hiding the pieces better. After a short trip, his father returned to find Ole's sailboat proudly slipped into a nearby lake.

Andrew gripped his ambitious son by the shoulder. "I'd hoped to make a farmer out of you," Andrew said, "but I guess you're cut out for something better, son. You've built a right nice boat."

Ole left the farm to become an apprentice machinist in Madison, Wis. Then he held a five-year string of odd jobs in the machine industry.

Eventually, Ole was attracted by the horseless carriage craze. "From the very first I needed a partner, and I knew it," he told a reporter. "My idea was to get somebody who could handle the business and leave me free to design and experiment."

But four attempts at partnerships fizzled.

Frustrated, Evinrude took his talents to the machine pattern-making business and became successful.

Bess Cary, a business school student who'd been typing letters for Evinrude all along, became the inventor's wife and partner. She was eight years younger than he.

It was Bess who insisted on a 10-day trial period for the new outboard motor. The daring move built consumer confidence.

As a woman in business in the early 1900s, Bess had to prove her mettle.

When two exporters who traveled to Milwaukee got over their shock at finding that the B. Evinrude of their correspondence was a woman, they and she hashed out a deal for 1,000 motors. The exporters later ordered 3,000 more motors and then an additional 5,000.

Although business boomed, Bess's health declined. Ole put marriage before business with two simple words: "We'll sell."

Ole sold Evinrude Motors in 1914, signed a five-year noncompete clause and took the family — Bess and son Ralph (born in 1907) — on an extended vacation.

Slowly, Bess's health improved, and Ole returned to the drawing board. As soon as the noncompete clause expired, Evinrude took a new motor, the Evinrude Light Twin Outboard, to Chris Meyer, his old friend and president of Evinrude Motors.

Meyer wasn't interested. He saw no need to retool Evinrude's original design.

But Ole knew that because of fierce competition the only way to stay afloat was to build a better motor. Ole's new firm, Elto Outboard Motor Co. of Milwaukee, soon pushed Evinrude to third place.

Both manufacturers chased a new leader, Johnson Motors, which had succeeded by stressing outboard racing. To compete, Ole devised the Super Elto Quad. At 35 miles per hour, it was faster and more appealing to consumers.

In early 1929, Elto merged with Evinrude and Lockwood Motor Co. to create Outboard Motor Corp. But seven months later, in October, the stock market crashed.

Ole put every resource into surviving the Depression. To meet payroll, the company held weekend factory sales of leftovers and motors made from extra spare parts. The competition scoffed, but OMC survived.

Bess didn't. In May 1933, she succumbed to her long-lingering health problems.

Fourteen months later, Bess's still-mourning husband also died.

"Alone, I don't believe I'd ever have amounted to much," Ole had told *The American Magazine* years earlier. "But together, Bess and I, we've done things." Outboard Motor Corp. changed its name in 1956 to Outboard Marine Corp. and is now based in Waukegan, Ill.

49

Statistician
W. Edwards Deming
His Push For High Quality Changed
The Corporate Approach

It was 1950, and American W. Edwards Deming was about to fire the first shot of a revolution. It was a shot heard 'round the world.

He'd gone to Japan to lecture engineers and executives on quality control.

The country was raising itself from the rubble of World War II. Industry had stalled. The economy was shattered.

But unlike American corporations that had turned a deaf ear to Deming's teachings, the Japanese were eager to listen and learn.

About 240 Japanese corporate leaders turned out — emptying nearly 80% of that country's top executive suites — for the momentous eight-day July seminar.

To make sure they got his message, Deming approached them in a manner entirely different from what they were accustomed to: The tall, crew-cut teacher stood in front of the business leaders, grabbed them by their mental lapels and sent traditional business notions flying into the air like bowling pins.

Tradition said high quality was expensive. Deming said that high quality actually lowered costs. Tradition defined the factory inspector as the overseer of quality. Deming said that by the time an inspector saw a finished product, it was too late. High quality, he argued, begins in the boardroom.

Tradition called maximum profits the result of a firm's minimizing costs and maximizing revenue. Deming said profits came from loyal — not just satisfied — customers.

The Japanese leaders drank it in. He'd shaken them up with his fire, and they loved him for it. To motivate them, Deming left them with a challenge: Their industries could be competitive with those in the West, provided they put his teachings into practice.

"I predicted in 1950 that in five years manufacturers the world over would be screaming for protection," Deming (1900–93) recounted of the Japanese experience. "It took only four years."

After Deming's lectures, according to Rafael Aguayo, author of *Dr. Deming: The American Who Taught the Japanese About Quality*, the leaders went back and downloaded Deming's philosophy into their companies like software.

Results soon followed. Names such as Toyota, Sony and Honda popped onto the world stage as symbols of quality. "Made in Japan" was no longer a joke. It was the new standard.

Deming's mission came full circle in 1980 when an NBC News television special called *If Japan Can, Why Can't We?* revealed the invisible and forgotten man behind the "Japanese industrial miracle." The prophet was suddenly with honor in his own country, and Fortune 500 companies sought out Deming's help.

One such firm was Ford Motor Co., whose backside was being kicked by the Japanese. Deming's series of lectures at Ford showed the company about high quality and creating continual improvement.

Ford adopted "Quality Is Job 1" as its mission statement in 1983, and three years later the Ford Taurus line sped into the lead position in the American auto market. Other Fortune 500 companies followed Ford's lead and hired Deming as a consultant.

"[Deming] had a huge effect on American industry. If you look at companies like General Electric, today they're doing [the quality-control program] Six Sigma. That's in part because of Deming," said Charles O'Reilley, a Stanford University Graduate School of Business professor and co-author of *Winning Through Innovation*.

Deming's quest for excellent quality was born in the hardship of his near-poverty-level upbringing. Born in Sioux City, Iowa, he was reared in Powell, Wyo. in a tarpaper shack. So meager was his family's existence that members sometimes prayed for food.

Deming was determined to beat poverty and made education his top priority. He graduated from high school in a class of 11. He worked odd jobs to pay for his bachelor's and master's degrees. Yale University took notice of this hard worker with high standards and offered him a scholarship for his doctoral degree in mathematical physics.

After graduation, he taught physics and then went to Washington, D.C., in 1930 as a researcher for the Agriculture Department.

Although he wrote nearly 40 scientific papers on physics, he discovered he was really passionate about how the statistics he used could affect other disciplines. His friendship with physicist Walter A. Shewhart proved key. At Bell Laboratories, Shewhart discovered statistical approaches to uniformity and quality in manufacturing and helped turn the American telephone system into the global standard.

Deming partnered with Shewhart to learn his methods. Together, the two physicists theorized that as quality in an operation improved, costs would actually go down.

They didn't just rely on numbers, however. Deming and Shewhart used common sense and their own experiences and examined organizations to see whether their theory held. It appeared it did.

Still, the pair's fresh thinking slammed head-on into prevailing notions that argued for emphasizing quantity, not quality. But Deming was sure he was right.

He looked for a way to prove it and got his chance in 1939 when he joined the Census Bureau as head statistician. Incorporating all he'd learned into the giant system, the bureau was able to crank out vastly more amounts of detailed data at a greatly reduced cost.

Finally recognized in his field, Deming taught quality control to 35,000 American engineers during World War II, instructing them how to use statistics to improve the quality of war materials. The Union of Japanese Scientists and Engineers took note of that work and after the war requested Deming come to Japan to teach his approach.

Deming relied on results to convince students. "Profits come from loyal customers," he said. "Loyal customers are created by offering high-quality products. Because only the customer can determine what a high-quality product is, the aim of business should be to find out what the customer wants."

"In the old days before the industrial era," Deming said, "the tailor, the carpenter, the shoemaker, the milkman and the blacksmith knew his customers by name. He knew whether they were satisfied and what he should do to improve his product."

Deming's counsel to modern business: "We have to present to [the customer] something he needs, in a way that he can use it. Study his needs; get ahead of him!"

Deming also stressed teamwork and cooperation, not competition, within a business.

Following his teachings, Japanese companies established quality circles so that workers could come together to suggest solutions to problems. Toyota workers, for instance, averaged 33 suggestions per worker per year, and about 90% of those were implemented, according to Aguayo. By the mid-1980s, quality circles were in place in about 90% of Fortune 500 firms.

Deming's sometimes-gruff nature reflected impatience with managerial abuses of power. He thought that power carried a precious responsibility. "Research shows," Deming said, "that the climate of an organization influences an individual's contribution far more than the individual himself."

He took some controversial positions. He charged that corporate obsession with profit was misplaced. A company that makes high quality the goal of everything it does is looking ahead, not in the rearview mirror.

"What is quality?" Deming once asked his MBA students in the first class of the year at New York University. "Quality," he answered himself, "is pride of workmanship."

50

Fashion Designer Coco Chanel
She Sewed Up Success

Gabrielle Chanel liked to sneak up into her aunt's attic and read romance novels. Inspired by the ornate settings and love-struck characters, she once labored for hours to make a garish dress of mauve crepe de chine and purple velvet.

When the teen-ager donned her creation for her school graduation, her aunt's horrified response taught her something she never forgot.

The lesson? In fashion, less is more. "Always remove, never add," Chanel said.

Chanel (1882–1971) never deviated from that rule during her decades-long career. While her personal life often overflowed with complexities, her signature clothing style was consistently simple and sophisticated.

She stuck single-mindedly to garments with clean lines, comfortable fits and no superfluous elements. Her suits, little black dresses, sling-back pumps, fragrances and faux jewelry are still in demand.

Her company, Paris-based Chanel SA, continues a booming business, some 30 years after her death. With couture and ready-to-wear designs by Karl Lagerfeld, the fashion house sells Chanel's classically tailored suits in 110 or so boutiques and high-end department stores.

The going price of a Chanel? About $5,000 as the 21st century got underway.

Synonymous With Success

A *Time* magazine obituary of Chanel upon her death said her name conjured up images of "prestige, quality, impeccable taste and unmistakable style."

Privately held, the firm she started in 1910 is owned by the Wertheimers, the same family that backed the launch of her perfume business in 1924. The company won't disclose current revenue, but reports peg it at $760 million in 1997.

Chanel's humble beginnings gave no indication of the success that would follow. Born into poverty, she was orphaned at 12 when her sickly mother died and her father abandoned her and her sister.

Other family members rejected the two girls, a fact that hurt Chanel deeply. She spent her teen years in an orphanage. The austere black uniforms and sparse surroundings left a deep, sad impression on Gabrielle.

But the girl decided never to let her heartache show. "Pride was the key to her character," wrote Janet Wallach, author of *Chanel: Her Style and Her Life.*

That pride revealed itself in her own clothing choices as she became a young woman. Since she couldn't afford the fashions of the times, she decided to create her own.

Pretty and petite, Chanel stood out in her simple white-collared dress and handmade straw hat. Women's clothes in the early 1900s were frilly and form fitting. Her goal was to be feminine but always relaxed and comfortable.

The loneliness of her childhood only fueled her drive to succeed on her own terms. "People laughed at the way I dressed, but that was the secret of my success. I didn't look like anyone," Marcel Haedrich quoted her in his book *Coco Chanel.*

Her nickname Coco, French for "little pet," might have come from her father. But Chanel preferred to keep a mysterious aura and told several versions of her life story. A tale has the name originating from a song she once sang at a café in Vichy, "Qui-qu'a-vu-Coco."

Chanel left the convent school at age 20. She lived with Etienne Balsan, a military officer. It was on his estate at Royallieu that she developed her own tastes for luxury.

She soon attracted the attention of Arthur "Boy" Capel, a wealthy English polo player, whom she lived with next. It was Capel who financed her first millinery in 1910, Chanel Modes, in Paris.

Chanel strove for originality. She made her hats unfussy, starkly different from the common frilly, feather-boa-topped hats of the day. She said about the usual styles worn by her peers, "How can a brain function under those things?"

She believed that formality in the workplace helped set a professional tone. Her staff addressed her as "Mademoiselle," and she called workers "Madame," "Mademoiselle" or "Monsieur" along with their last names.

Her work routines demonstrated her unique focus. She didn't do standard design drawings but cut fabric directly on customers and models.

She found inspiration in the everyday clothes she saw around her and innovated, says www.fashionwindows.com editor Boyd Davis. She borrowed ideas "from a mechanic's blouse, a ditch digger's scarf, and the white collar and cuffs of a waitress," he wrote.

Chanel "appropriated" men's clothing of her day, including sports jackets, turning them into functional feminine hybrids, wrote the editor of *Interview* magazine, Ingrid Sischy. Chanel is credited with popularizing bobbed hair, boyish flapper styles and trousers for women.

"Sometimes the determining factor was practicality: Chanel wore bell-bottom trousers in Venice, the better to climb in and out of gondolas, and started the pants revolution," reported *Time*.

Marketing Queen

She wore her own creations always to advertise them. To appeal to a wide audience of women, she kept offering them alternatives to the usual looks. The *Times of London*'s Emily Davies wrote, "If ever there was a marketing queen before her time, it was Gabrielle Chanel."

Chanel knew that appearances were important, and a good address was one of them. As she used her social life to attract well-heeled clients, she took up residence at the Ritz Carleton hotel in Paris. There, she'd often host salons with famous artists of her day.

Composer Igor Stravinksy and his family lived with her for a time. Pablo Picasso and choreographer Diaghilev were her friends. Her clientele grew and included Hollywood elite and international royalty: Princess Grace, Queen Fabiola and Marlene Dietrich, for example.

Chanel's life was not without controversy. She closed her business in 1939 when France declared war on Germany. She was then exiled to Switzerland in 1945 for a relationship with a Nazi officer, Hans Gunther von Dincklage.

But Chanel wasn't one to give up her dream. She kept creating fashions and finally staged a successful comeback in Paris in 1954. Some say she was goaded into returning to work by her distaste for Christian Dior's pinched-waist looks.

51

Innovator Joseph C. Wilson

His Determination Built Xerox Into A Billion-Dollar Company

Joseph C. Wilson saw opportunities where his competitors saw only folly.

Wilson (1909–71) was president of Haloid Co., a Rochester, N.Y., family-owned business that had developed a superior photocopy paper.

Still, as Peter Krass wrote in *The Book of Entrepreneurs' Wisdom*, Wilson "realized for his company to survive, [it] would need to diversify into new products, so he ordered his research chief [John Dessauer] to keep abreast of any interesting inventions or patents."

During his search, Dessauer heard about a new electrophotographic process for making copies of documents that was being developed in Columbus, Ohio. Interested, Dessauer and Wilson went there to investigate.

There, they met with inventor-lawyer Chester F. Carlson. Carlson had tried, unsuccessfully, to interest almost two dozen major concerns in the process. None saw any potential in the system, which used electric charges to get ink to adhere to paper.

But Wilson was different. He saw possibilities in the process, which became more popularly known as *xerography*. His willingness to take a risk helped Haloid grow into a billion-dollar company — now known as Xerox Corp.

Wilson was born in Rochester, attended the University of Rochester and went on to Harvard Business School, where he earned an MBA. Although he loved to learn and briefly considered an academic career, his relatives urged him to join the family firm in 1933 as an assistant to the sales manager.

Gearing up to do his best in that arena, too, Wilson quickly worked his way up the ranks. In 1936, after Haloid purchased a controlling interest in the Rectigraph Co., which manufactured early photocopy machines, Wilson was put in charge of Rectigraph.

He was a strong believer in customer satisfaction. To make sure customers were happy, he quickly set up a sales and service organization for Rectigraph, which was unusual in that field at the time.

"It is the customer and the customer alone who will ultimately determine whether we succeed or fail as a company," Wilson often said.

He also began to hire new employees who were open to the possibilities of change. As he said in an employee orientation speech around 1963: "We are a company which pays a premium on imagination, on the use of creativity, on the use of brains to think of new ideas. We do not want to do things the same old way. Therefore, as you come here, I hope that you come with an attitude that change will be a way of life for you. You will not do things tomorrow the way you are doing them today."

Wilson didn't. He looked constantly for new challenges himself, also hoping to inspire his employees.

"To set high goals, to have almost unattainable aspirations, to imbue people with the belief that they can be achieved — these are as important as the balance sheet, perhaps more so," he said when asked how he saw his role at the company.

Wilson became aware of the xerographic process in 1946, around the time he was named president of the company. It was a difficult period for the firm.

Haloid's revenue had increased during World War II and was just under $7 million in 1946, compared with $1.4 million in 1936. Because of competitive price pressures, though, profits had dropped to around $150,000 in 1946 from a peak of $300,000 in 1939.

Wilson knew the dangers of financing extensive development of the untried copy process, particularly at a time when profits were declining.

But he believed in the process and was certain that it held great potential.

Others thought he was crazy. Developing xerography was a lengthy and complicated process that turned out to be more expensive than anyone imagined. As Wilson wrote in an article for *Nation's Business,* "For every technical problem we solved, we encountered another for which we had no answer."

Still, Wilson stayed committed to the process and kept pushing his researchers forward. Between 1950 and 1959, for example, the company spent more than $12 million on developing xerography — exceeding its profits from those years.

In fact, the situation became so iffy at one point that Wilson lent some of his personal funds to the company to keep it going.

The company introduced its first Xerox machine in 1949, a nonautomatic copier. It was a crowded marketplace, with numerous and large competitors. Eastman Kodak Co., for example, was pushing a process it called "Verifax"; Minnesota Mining & Manufacturing Co. sold a system called "Thermofax."

Typically at the time, the photocopying industry operated in a manner similar to the razor business — that is, it virtually gave away the razor and made its money on the blades. With photocopiers, 85% of the manufacturers' income came from selling customers supplies such as special ink and paper, and only 15% came from selling the machines themselves.

But that wasn't an option at Haloid: The early xerographic machines used plain paper but were sophisticated and expensive to manufacture. "I don't think 10% of them would have been sold," Wilson said.

So he had to come up with an alternative. "You cannot make much progress by following conventional guidelines," he said.

Instead of selling his machines, he leased them. Users paid a fee that covered the machine and a certain number of copies. Beyond that first batch, the fee per copy lessened.

Wilson said the decision "had some serious disadvantages. It required a lot of capital. And it provided that we absorb all the risk of obsolescence, our customers none. It took a lot of faith, but it was absolutely essential — just as important as getting into xerography itself — to have chosen that particular method in the early stages."

By 1957, the company had become so identified with the process it changed its name to Haloid-Xerox, and in 1960, the name was changed again to Xerox. Also in 1960, the company began to sell its first automatic copier, the 914 (so named because it could copy sheets as large as 9 by 14 inches).

It was a quantum leap forward in photocopying technology. Earlier Xerox machines were complicated to operate. Some early machines were sold with fire extinguishers because they occasionally turned paper to ash.

Now Wilson faced the task of convincing potential but skeptical users that the 914 was a revolutionary product. Why not entertain customers into buying one?

To show customers how easy the 914 was to use, Xerox trained a chimpanzee to make it work.

The 914 became the breakthrough product Wilson hoped it would be. Xerox sales jumped from about $60 million in 1961 to $180 million in 1967; it was a billion-dollar corporation in 1971.

Throughout this period, Wilson tried to keep workers as focused on their interior lives as they were on the company's products.

"The whole purpose of Xerox is to offer profitable innovations in fields to which we attribute social value and human need," he said in a 1967 speech to investment analysts in Chicago. "We encourage Xerox people to involve themselves in issues of importance. We cannot as individuals or as a corporation isolate ourselves in a vacuum."

52

Inventor John Mauchly

His Determination Helped Launch
The Computer Age

John Mauchly wanted to rip up his employment contract. "I am distinctly unhappy because my usefulness to Remington Rand has become severely circumscribed," he wrote to his boss in 1952.

"At present I am just punching an adding machine on a problem which deserves a Univac. That isn't progress."

It was classic Mauchly (1907–80), refusing to accept the status quo and constantly searching for better ways to do things.

Mauchly never sent the letter. But even if he never worked another day, Mauchly had already launched the world on its course to the computer age.

Mauchly wrote a paper in 1941 that was the genesis of ENIAC, the first modern computer. He also co-developed the Univac, the first mass-produced computer. And he pioneered the field of software programming, which spurred the use of computers for business.

Mauchly shares credit for inventing the ENIAC and the Univac with John Presper Eckert Jr. (1919–95). Eckert was the engineer and Mauchly the visionary.

The son of a physicist, Mauchly absorbed his father's interest in that field and decided to emulate him. He received a doctorate in physics from Johns Hopkins University in 1932. But his specialty, molecular spectroscopy, didn't attract the top research institutions at the time. The hot field was nuclear physics.

It was tough finding good jobs during the Depression, but Mauchly had a flexible outlook. He took a job teaching introductory physics at Ursinus College, a small liberal-arts school outside Philadelphia.

To stay sharp, Mauchly was also doing research in meteorology, which required intense calculations. But Ursinus College lacked the cutting-edge equipment of leading laboratories at the time. So Mauchly decided to improvise: He began experimenting with newer and faster ways to perform complex calculations, including work on electrical circuits.

Seeking to expand his own experience so he'd have more to offer, Mauchly enrolled in a course at the Moore School for Electrical Engineering at the University of Pennsylvania — even though he already had a doctorate. He joined a team assigned to improve the accuracy of missile trajectories for the U.S. military.

Their primary calculating tool was made of electric motors, shafts, wheels and handles. The calculations could take weeks to complete. But Mauchly believed there had to be a way to do it in days, even minutes.

His ideas were covered in a five-page memo titled "The Use of Vacuum Tube Devices in Calculating." The paper was ignored, except by Eckert, one of the brightest electronic engineers at Moore. Realizing they might learn from each other, the two spent hours discussing how to build and use electronics for high-speed computing.

"He and I talked about this idea in the back-of-the-envelope stage, made little sketches on bits and hunks of paper when we'd go out to lunch together," Eckert said in an interview in 1988.

Despite scoffing by others, Mauchly and Eckert pushed their ideas. Finally they caught the attention of a military officer who helped persuade the government to fund a project to build the first electronic digital computer. It was called the Electronic Numerical Integrator and Computer.

Electronics was in its infancy. Some professors at Moore, where ENIAC was built, didn't want to be associated with the project because they thought it wouldn't work.

Mauchly's confidence never waned. To motivate others helping with the project, he continually reassured them that they were visionaries who were making history. One of the programmers later said: "John constantly pushed me to think beyond the present task and toward the future."

Kay Mauchly Antonelli, Mauchly's widow and an original ENIAC programmer, says her husband pushed people to think beyond what they believed possible.

"He once gave me this book, called *Wake Up and Live*. He would tell me to look all around and see what alternatives there are. Nothing is a dead end," she said in a 2001 interview.

Unveiled in 1946, ENIAC was a behemoth with more than 16,000 vacuum tubes and 6,000 manual switches. Among other things, it was used to develop the hydrogen bomb.

Ever the optimist, Mauchly believed he could build an even better computer. He and Eckert formed a company in Philadelphia, with Eckert working mostly on the computer design while Mauchly developed programs to expand its use.

Math professors and scientific naysayers questioned the practicality of such a machine. Some believed there would never be a need for more than a few of them.

"Nobody believed in them," said Antonelli. "They were operating on a shoestring, but they had big ideas."

Mauchly wasn't one to walk away from a challenge. "I have a stubborn streak," he once said in an interview. "If others say this can't be solved, to me it's a challenge to ask why. Let's examine this further."

As Eckert and Mauchly worked on their new computer, the Census Bureau needed help monitoring the exploding U.S. population. It signed on Eckert and Mauchly to build the Universal Automatic Computer. Work on the Univac began.

Though gifted engineers, Eckert and Mauchly were inept at managing costs and were running out of money. They continued working, though, believing that even if they lost money on the first Univac, the experience would open the door to more orders.

Matters took an unexpected turn when the untimely death of an investor allowed Remington Rand Corp. to acquire 40% of the company. Remington Rand, best known for electric shavers, bought additional stock held by employees, ultimately gaining 51% of Eckert-Mauchly Corp.

Eckert and Mauchly, in dire financial straits, finally agreed to sell their shares to Remington Rand in 1950, and both signed 10-year contracts. Work on the Univac proceeded.

Remington built 46 Univac 1 computers. The government bought the first seven; General Electric Co. bought the eighth, for payroll services. The world of business computing was under way.

Mauchly stood his ground when he believed in something. Take the time when his car was seen near an anti-nuclear rally during a trip to Washington, D.C. It was the era of McCarthyism and the "Red Scare." Mauchly was investigated on suspicion of being a communist, blacklisted by the government and fired by Remington.

Refusing to back down, Mauchly fought the charges for two years. He won and rejoined the company.

Determined to continue his work, Mauchly worked on programming during his two-year exile from the company. To stay ahead, he hired Grace Hopper, who would later invent Cobol, one of the most popular and widespread computer programs ever.

"He was forever a teacher. He shared everything with everybody," Antonelli said.

Mauchly left the company, which would ultimately become a part of Unisys Corp., when his 10-year contract expired. It was time, he said, to explore new avenues.

According to the University of Pennsylvania, which maintains documents on Mauchly's research, he built a machine that inherently served more applications than he could possibly envision. A market emerged for people who could provide advice on the use of computers.

And Mauchly had stayed up to date with trends. Seeing that computer use would flourish, he set up his own consulting firm. In the late 1960s, he shifted his focus toward project planning and management techniques. He served as a consultant, returning to the life of an independent thinker.

53

Inventor Howard Head

His Determination Revolutionized
The Way We Ski And Play Tennis

Howard Head despised the concept of marketing. The best way to appeal to the masses, he thought, was simple: Come up with the best product.

"I think marketing is a dirty word. I've never liked it," Head told students at Harvard Business School in 1988. "Get it right, and the product will sell itself."

Head proved his point by designing and mass-producing the first composite skis in the early 1950s. Why did the sleek black Head skis schuss past the competition? They made skiing easier and more fun.

"No discussion of the American ski scene would be complete without a reappraisal of the Head Ski, the metal-plastic sandwich that revolutionized ski making," *SKI Magazine* wrote in 1953. "Its wonderfully easy skiing characteristics have given it a firm and secure place in the affections of almost everybody."

Head (1914–91) made a fortune through the Head Ski Co., which he sold in 1969 for $16 million. Seven years later, Head stunned the sports world again with the Prince tennis racquet, the first oversized racquet to achieve commercial success. Some of the world's best tennis players, including Jennifer Capriati and Australia's Patrick Rafter, have competed with Prince gear.

In hindsight, the composite ski and the oversized racquet seemed so obvious. Why was Head the first to come up with both? He was disgusted with what was available on the market and acted on it.

Head, who began his career as an aircraft engineer, took up skiing after World War II. The Philadelphia native quickly found he wasn't good at it. His all-wood skis, he realized, made it very hard to maneuver. If wood were still the best material with which to make skis, Head reckoned, they'd still build airplanes from it.

"I think creativity comes from dissatisfaction, rather than trying to invent something," he said. "It's a nitpickiness that cannot sit still if you see something that can be improved."

Head quit his job at Glenn L. Martin Co. and focused on making a better ski. Using $6,000 in poker winnings, he rented the corner of an electrical appliance shop in Baltimore in the summer of 1947.

Head molded his first skis from aluminum, plastic and plywood. To fuse the materials together, he placed all the parts in a big rubber bag, pumped all the air out to create pressure, and dumped the bag inside a trough of oil heated to 350 degrees.

By January 1948, Head had made six pairs of skis. He took them to teachers at Stowe Ski School in Vermont. All six broke simply by flexing.

He went back to his shop and made a ski as strong as wood with half the weight. But ski teachers who tried them complained that snow caked along the bottom. The ski edges also dulled too fast.

Head refused to give up. When he ran out of money, he borrowed from friends. He was so convinced he was on the right track that he persuaded his production team to stay on without pay. Together they continued to innovate, using new materials, new manufacturing methods and new designs.

Finally Head came up with his 40th version, nearly as heavy as wood skis. He added a plastic layer for slipperiness, a plywood core for strength and high-carbon steel edges. The skis were flexible yet hard to twist, allowing skiers to carve their turns.

He took them to instructor Clif Taylor, who whooshed down a mountain cliff in Vermont and carved pretty turns one spring day in 1950. Head knew this time he'd gotten it right.

To gain widespread acceptance of his products, Head listened carefully to customers.

From 1950 to 1957, sales of Head skis grew from 300 pairs to 27,000. Then growth dovetailed. Pro racers refused to use them because they didn't hold on turns at racing speed. They flapped and chattered too much on hardpack and rutted courses.

Head took the criticism to heart and started experimenting again. In 1955, he patented a neoprene rubber layer and introduced a one-piece L-shaped racing edge, adding more raw strength.

"Don't sit around thinking," Head said at a Harvard Business School lecture. "Do it, cut it, try it, make it work. Find a solution."

Success didn't come easily at all for Head. He went to Harvard University aiming to become a creative writer but nearly flunked his writing classes. An aptitude test showed he had talent for "structural visualization."

Head changed his major to engineering, and the decision paid off. After graduating in 1936, he went to work at Glenn L. Martin Co., the predecessor of Martin Marietta, as a riveter. He couldn't read a blueprint, but from the first day of work Head knew he was in the right field.

"On that first day, I found out the joy of work," Head said.

After retiring from the ski business, Head took up tennis. Again, he found the sport tougher than he'd thought.

Head's tennis teacher recommended he buy a ball machine from Prince Manufacturing Co. in Princeton, N.J. The device intrigued him so much that he called the company to share ideas on how to improve it. He ended up buying a large chunk of the firm for $27,000. Head also became its chief engineer.

Within a year, Head fixed the machine's kinks. Sales grew hot. But it still didn't improve Head's tennis. So he focused his energies on making a better racquet.

Head put weights at opposite ends of the racquet. That didn't work. Why not increase the racquet's hitting area while keeping the weight the same?

By making the racquet wider and pulling the throat down closer to the handle, Head's team produced a racquet with a 60% larger hitting area. The result? A sweet spot 3½ times bigger than that of an ordinary wood racquet. Now, players could strike the ball despite hitting it off-center.

Head's Prince racquet, which made its debut in 1976, met lots of critics. Veteran teacher Vic Braden said, "the only difference the Prince racket makes is that now when you serve, you will hit both your legs rather than just one," according to a Harvard Business School case study.

Head ignored the critics and approached pro players to try his racquet. In 1978, young Pam Shriver, wielding a Prince, beat Martina Navratilova to reach the U.S. Open women's final. The racquets quickly caught on. Sales mushroomed from $3 million in 1976 to $34 million in 1981, when Prince dominated the high-end racquet market.

Head challenged others to do their best. Why? He sincerely wanted to make a better product. He never took "No" for an answer, says Malcolm Bash, who was head of manufacturing at Prince Tennis.

Head often called Bash at weird hours, asking him to test a new idea and get back to him within a few hours. When Bash said it couldn't be done, Head insisted. In the end, Bash would come up with a working solution.

"He had a vision, and always knew what he wanted, and you couldn't stand in his way," Bash said. "I found him to be a real inspiration."

54

Intel Co-founder Robert Noyce

He Invented His Way To The Top

Robert Noyce thought the best way to make a leap forward was to give talented people the tools they needed and then get out of the way.

Noyce, a co-founder of Fairchild Semiconductor and Intel, saw his job this way: "People come here [to Intel] because of their abilities. My job [is] to remove all impediments to progress and give them as much freedom as possible."

Noyce (1928–90) was a brilliant scientist who created the modern integrated circuit, considered by some one of the most important inventions in history.

He received the National Medal of Science (1980), was inducted into the National Inventor's Hall of Fame (1983), won the National Medal of Technology (1987) and was awarded the Charles Scott Draper Award, engineering's Nobel Prize (1990).

He also became a great manager who encouraged those who worked for him with his positive attitude.

"Optimism is an essential ingredient for innovation," Noyce wrote in *Innovation for Prosperity: The Coming Decade.*

"How else can the individual welcome change over security, adventure over staying in safe places? Innovation cannot be mandated any more than a baseball coach can demand that the next batter hit a home run. He can, however, assemble a good team, encourage his players and play the odds."

No Slave To Convention

Noyce never felt tied to conventional wisdom. "He would just suggest things that were absolutely contrary to the scientific knowledge of the time," said Gordon Moore, a founding partner of Fairchild Semiconductors and Intel. "And he succeeded in making major advances in the technology 10 years before the industry understood the physics that made it happen."

For instance, Moore told *IEEE Spectrum*, the publication of the Institute of Electrical and Electronics Engineers, he recalled struggling during his Fairchild days "to find one metal that would make contact with both the emitter and the base" of a transistor. Noyce suggested he try aluminum.

"As a physicist, it was contrary to all he knew," Moore said. "But it worked."

Noyce, born in Burlington, Iowa, was something of a physics prodigy. He took college-level courses while still in high school and majored in both physics and math at Grinnell College.

In school, he was greatly influenced by physics professor Grant Gale. Friends of Gale developed the first transistor at Bell Labs and sent him early samples, which he showed to Noyce's class. Transistors entranced Noyce. He enrolled at the Massachusetts Institute of Technology to pursue further studies in the field.

Ironically, transistor technology was so newfangled it "was still considered a novelty" at the school, according to a commemorative book Intel issued after Noyce's death.

But Noyce had a vision of the future, and there were no vacuum tubes in it. So while he completed his traditional course work, he kept his eye on the early innovative work being done in transistors and semiconductors.

Noyce set a goal for himself: He wanted to be an active participant in original research. After earning his doctorate, he was offered many jobs with prestigious companies such as IBM, RCA and General Electric.

Instead, he chose to work for Philco, the company that offered the lowest salary. "It was a little group, and I felt [it] needed me very badly," he told *IEEE Spectrum.*

From there he joined William Shockley. Shockley had managed the Bell Labs project that created the transistor and left to form his own company, Shockley Semiconductor Laboratories. But Shockley proved a better scientist than manager, and seven disgruntled scientists left him to form a new company, which became Fairchild Semiconductors. They convinced Noyce to join them.

The company was successful almost from the beginning but eventually, to Noyce's thinking, became a victim of its success. Fairchild Camera exercised its option to buy the company and took firm control, running it from its East Coast headquarters.

Antipathy Toward Bureaucracy

Noyce came away from his experience at Fairchild with an antipathy for bureaucratic organization, according to *BusinessWeek.*

Because of the parent company's management style, Noyce felt it increasingly difficult to initiate new projects. That's what ultimately persuaded Noyce and Moore, in 1968, to start Intel (for "integrated electronics").

Both had enough confidence in their ability to make it work that they put up $250,000 each as seed money.

Setting up the new business, Noyce was determined to learn from the mistakes he'd seen at Fairchild. Intel was based on a "no-frills, egalitarian management style," *BusinessWeek* wrote.

He immediately did away with symbols of rank. There were no reserved parking spots at Intel, no private offices.

Noyce tried to keep the decision-making process simple and quick. Major decisions "were not bucked up a chain of command," Tom Wolfe wrote. "Noyce held weekly meetings with people from all parts of the operation, and whatever had to be worked out was worked out right there in the room."

55

GE's Jack Welch

His Innovation Sealed The Company's Success

Jack Welch launched a revolution at General Electric Co. by drawing three circles on a pad of paper.

The company's new chief executive illustrated his battle plan in 1982 to fellow GE executive James Baughman. Welch was going to transform GE from lumbering Goliath to agile David.

The three circles represented the sectors Welch felt were GE's bright future: services, core businesses and high technology. Inside the circles Welch placed 15 GE winners such as aircraft engines, lighting, medical systems, plastics and information services.

Outside the circles he placed the also-rans: GE central air conditioning and the popular but dowdy housewares. Welch offered these companies one of three fates: "Fix, close or sell."

If this natural selection seems brutal, so was the foreign competition in the 1970s and 1980s that had grabbed U.S. market share in autos and steel — turf long considered almost an American entitlement. Business was going global. Competition was feverish. GE's 350 businesses, 600 profit centers and 12 layers of management needed a shakeup.

Welch believed he was the man to do it.

"I want a revolution at GE. Let's go for it," Welch told an executive the day after Welch took the reins at GE in 1981, wrote Robert Slater in *The New GE*.

By building on GE's strong suits, he aimed to turn the company, founded in 1878 by Thomas Alva Edison, into the most competitive operation on earth. "We believe this central idea — being No. 1 or No. 2 [in each of GE's business segments] — more than an objective, a requirement, will give us a set of businesses which will be unique in the world business equation," Welch said.

Enemies of his undertaking could be found within and without. Inside was bureaucracy. Outside was tough overseas competition.

"[That bureaucracy] was right for its time, but the times were changing rapidly," Welch said. "Change was occurring at a much faster pace than business was reacting to it."

So Welch delivered the changes. They were jolting. By 1984, he'd jettisoned 150 GE businesses worth more than $5 billion. By 1986, he'd axed 130,000 jobs — a quarter of the company's personnel. But returns for 1985 proved he was on the right track. That year, GE was the fifth-most-profitable U.S. company, Slater says.

Some critics take into account more than GE's strong numbers, though, in evaluating Welch's career. James J. O'Toole, a professor at the University of Southern California's Marshall School of Business who wrote about Welch in his book *Leadership A to Z*, says that Welch's leadership missed the mark in one significant area.

"I think there is also a moral component to leadership and that moral component has to do with gratitude to your followers, how they are treated, viewing the organization as something larger than merely a moneymaking machine. I think Welch very clearly ignored that aspect of it," O'Toole said.

But the crux of Welch's revolution involved retooling employees' mind-sets.

"We are trying to get the soul and energy of a start-up into the body of a $60 billion, 114-year-old company," he said. "We must have every good idea from every man and woman in the organization; we cannot afford management styles that suppress and intimidate."

Welch asked GE managers to approach their jobs through a fresh set of eyes. One senior manager, told by Welch that his sector was underperforming, asked Welch for help.

"What I'd like you to do is take a month off and just go away," Welch said, according to Slater. "Come back and act as if you were just assigned to the business and you hadn't been running it for four years. And you just want to come in brand new, hold all the reviews and start slicing everything in a different way."

He assigned his senior team members tough goals and kept close track of their progress during the year.

The three vice chairmen and the heads of GE's 12 business units who reported to him directly received handwritten two-page performance evaluations each year. He often popped in unexpectedly to visit their various GE operations. He also tethered all GE businesses to the Internet.

Besides adding billions of dollars in new businesses, Welch fostered a company culture for GE's next CEO to turn to when Welch retired in September 2001. Welch started or expanded programs such as the GE Management Development Institute at Crotonville, N.Y. — now known as the John F. Welch Leadership Center — Work Out, Best Practices, and Six Sigma to keep GE well defined and at the cutting edge. The company spends more than $1 billion a year educating its employees.

"Real communication," Welch told company workers in 1987, "is an attitude, an environment. It's the most interactive of all processes. It requires countless hours of eyeball-to-eyeball back and forth. It involves more listening than talking. It is a constant, interactive process aimed at creating consensus."

The company's Management Development Institute is one such consensus builder. Here the Welch philosophy is taught in courses such as "The New Manager" and "Applied Creative Thinking."

Welch inaugurated Work Out to open lines of communication among GE's people. Here problems and solutions bubble to the surface. Work Out brings managers and workers from all over the company into groups of 50 for three days of talking together.

Case in point: The editor of a popular plant newspaper stood up at one Work Out session and said it took her seven signatures to release each issue.

"Why does it take seven signatures?" she asked. Her manager, sitting nearby responded: "This is crazy. I didn't know that was the case. From now on, no more signatures."

Welch demanded direct and honest communication from these sessions. "These meetings are predicated on a belief that the people closest to the work know it best and are best qualified to make it better," said Welch in *Jack Welch Speaks,* by Janet Lowe. "[They are a] relentless, endless companywide search for a better way to do everything we do."

To keep new ideas flowing, Welch designed Best Practices, a program that helps workers look outside GE for inspiration. Company teams are sent for two weeks to high-performing companies to learn how they do things. Visited companies, in turn, send teams to GE.

For 20 years as GE's CEO, Welch was in constant improvement mode. In 1995 he launched the Six Sigma program to find defects in GE processes and pare them to as close to zero as possible. Tens of thousands of GE workers were trained in this statistical approach. It saved GE hundreds of millions of dollars and surpassed Welch's expectations.

Welch looked at his role as that of a facilitator.

"My job," he said, "is to put the best people on the biggest opportunities and the best allocation of dollars in the right places. That's about it. Transfer ideas and allocate resources and get out of the way."

In the end, Welch strove for simplicity. "You can't believe how hard it is for people to be simple, how much they fear being simple. They worry that if they're simple, people will think they're simple-minded. In reality, of course, it's just the reverse. Clear, tough-minded people are the most simple," he said.

Index

About *Investor's Business Daily*

Investor's Business Daily provides critical, no-nonsense finance and investing information to nearly a million readers every day. Known for its innovative approach and straightforward analysis, it's one of today's most essential tools for empowering individual and institutional investors. Visit online at www.investors.com.